The Terrifying Wind

Seeking Shelter Following the Death of a Child

Judith Sullivan

ISBN: 978-0-9895672-3-7

Library of Congress Control Number: 2013942917

Cover Image: Dark stormy Sea Waters at Night©istockphoto.com/fpm

The following permissions for material in this book are granted by:

From THE UNDERTAKING: Life Studies From the Dismal Trade by Thomas Lynch. ©1997 by Thomas Lynch. Used by permission of W.W. Norton & Company, Inc.

Adapted from BLACK SECONDS by Karin Fossum. Copyright ©2002 by Karin Fossum. English translation ©2007 by Charlotte Barslund. Used by permission of Houghton Mifflin Harcourt Publishing Company. All rights reserved.

SMALL MERCIES by Barbara McCauley. ©Barbara McCauley. Used by permission of Sherman Asher Publishing.

Excerpt from LEARNING TO FALL: THE BLESSINGS OF AN IMPERFECT LIFE by Philip Simmons, ©2002 by Philip Simmons. Used by permission of Bantam Books, an imprint of The Random House Publishing Group, a division of Random House LLC. All rights reserved. Any third party use of this material, outside of this publication, is prohibited. Interested parties must apply directly to Random House LLC for permission.

Excerpt from THE YEAR OF MAGICAL THINKING by Joan Didion, copyright ©2005 by Joan Didion. Used by permission of Alfred A. Knopf, an imprint of the Knopf Doubleday Publishing Group, a division of Random House LLC. All rights reserved. Any third party use of this material, outside of this publication, is prohibited. Interested parties must apply directly to Random House LLC for permission.

From HOW TO GO ON LIVING WHEN SOMEONE YOU LOVE DIES by Therese Rando, PhD. ©Therese Rando. Used by permission from Dr. Therese Rando. All rights reserved.

From CONTINUING BONDS: NEW UNDERSTANDINGS OF GRIEF by Dennis Klass, Phyllis R. Silverman, and Steven Nickman. Used by permission from the Copyright Clearance Center.

From TERRY: MY DAUGHTER'S LIFE-AND-DEATH STRUGGLE WITH ALCOHOLISM by George McGovern. ©George McGovern. Published by Penguin Group. All rights reserved.

Melissa's Garden Publishing

Table of Contents

III. Life Support

IV. Equilibrium and Transformation

For Melissa, Brandon, and John

But who among us gets to dictate the terms of his or her good fortune? You can't live for very long on this earth without confronting a fundamental truth: we're not in charge here, at least not entirely so. Our greatest blessings, along with our greatest burdens, seem to fall upon us unbidden. For all our planning, for all our talk of goals, for all our strategy and vision and commitment, we learn that many of our lives' most important events can't be predicted or controlled.

—Philip Simmons, *Learning to Fall*

Introduction

In December of 2001, my twenty-five-year-old daughter Melissa suffered a cardiac arrest and became comatose. The trauma occurred suddenly and unpredictably. She died twelve days later leaving my husband John and me in despair and hopelessness. During that time, however, a phenomenal movement began to take form as people from different parts of our lives reached out to us in our pain. Their collective actions became a kind of "life support" for us. Over time, we noticed that the potency of the support seemed to be generated by its closeness and constancy. Some individuals stayed close with scheduled predictability, while many others offered their support in more spontaneous ways. These experiences as a whole affected us profoundly, and we felt an overwhelming desire to write about them. We hoped that by doing so, those who would like to offer support to others in grief, especially those who have lost a child, might benefit from reading about our experience.

For several months after Melissa died John and I intermittently wrote down some of our ideas. Then John's professional responsibilities increased, preventing him from further writing. I decided to pick up the project and complete it. As I did so, I broadened the context to include the story of Melissa's death, what it felt like, a description of my grief and how it evolved over time. Most importantly, I wrote about how various kinds of life support helped throughout this process. In the end, the book covered a full decade of my grief experience.

It was hard to open up about my grief. I am not a person who easily discloses deep personal thoughts and feelings, so writing about the most profound pain of my life was a significant challenge. Yet each time I hesitated in my resolve, I only had to remember how our "life support" helped save us, and I resumed my efforts. I also had a professional motivation to stay focused and complete the book. As a psychotherapist, I realized that I could try to use my experiences to make a contribution to the understanding of grief.

In addition to confronting my own reserved nature, I also battled the constraints imposed by language. I quickly learned that words and phrases seemed inadequate when writing about our daughter's death and its aftermath. I often found myself in the shallow waters of scripted and stereotyped language of loss and grief even though I was drowning in complex feelings. Nevertheless, the deeper I allowed myself to go into my unique experience the more I felt I had emerged with insights others might find helpful.

In the end I am glad it took several years to write the book. This time allowed me to experience and to observe the evolution of my grief. Eventually, I was able to step beyond preoccupation with pain and reflect on what it might have been like to be one of our life supporters. It is clear that it is not a role for the faint of heart. It requires coming close to a pain that is bigger than any person thinks they can handle. It requires an understanding that nothing one does or says can take away or diminish the monstrous event. It means recognizing and acknowledging that profound human bonds have been ripped apart. Yet, when others joined us as we quaked before the absolute power of death, they were unknowingly lending us strength and courage when we had none of our own.

I have learned that my grief will never leave me. I wouldn't want it to, despite the pain. I have also learned that its remains will be scattered among all the other moments of my life, even the pleasant ones. That is how I tolerate it as a life sentence. Some memories are hypnotic, floating slowly toward me like snowflake crystals on a sunny winter's day. Other memories threaten to overwhelm me when I'm unprepared. In those moments the white flakes turn to ash.

In spite of my loss, I consider myself fortunate to be able to appreciate simple and ordinary things. There was a time when sorrow trumped every perspective and every other emotion. However, my capacity to feel love and affection for others has returned and grown. I can even feel joy at times. I can experience humor and laughter. I have discovered that more and more aspects of the world around me are fascinating, beautiful, and creative. I am especially grateful for the natural world, an abundant resource of transcendence for me.

All of the experiences described in the book, including reactions, feelings, and the grief process itself are mine unless otherwise stated. Every person's loss and circumstance are unique. I would not want to suggest it should be otherwise. I believe it is important for those who wish to be life supporters to realize this as well.

I am aware that some of you reading this book may be bereaved parents. I know the pain of loss you carry is probably the worst of your life. I hope you will find this book to be an acknowledgment of your grief and an affirmation of the tremendous courage and effort it takes to keep moving forward.

Grief Tale: One

There was a woman once who lived happily in the forest, among the trees and berry bushes. During one very special year on a sunny summer solstice she delivered a baby daughter. The child was impish, clever, kind, and strong, and remained so as she grew to become a young woman. Her hair flowed as the color of prairie grass in August and her eyes were the blue of a warm sea. A few freckles speckled her nose and cheeks. She always appeared younger than her actual age.

One day the woman complained about a minor event in her life. Her daughter said, "Oh, cry me a river!" The woman was taken aback by this lack of sympathy from her usually understanding daughter, but then she found herself smiling. From then on the woman was able to laugh at herself whenever she made things more serious than they really were.

Years later on an ordinary Friday morning in December her daughter suddenly died. Standing alone in the forest the woman watched as the sun turned dark and the wind stopped blowing. Then the sky took on the shape of a monstrous beast that roared and flashed its fiery eyes, daring her to look. As she did, the wind awoke in a terrifying fury, driving cold dark rain as sharp as icicles down at the woman. It pierced her body and stabbed her eyes. In great pain and partially blinded she stumbled along the path back to her cottage.

The next day she walked to a clearing in the woods and sat down.

Huge tears, the size of ponds, began to leak from her eyes. The tears flowed day after day and night after night. At first the woman thought she would dry up and would no longer exist, but then she realized that she, in fact, was crying a river. This time she did not laugh. Each day the same thing happened and the woman began to think she would drown. As time passed her huge tears deepened the river. Her hair grew very long, her eyes appeared not to see and the corners of her mouth almost reached her chin. Gradually the water rose beneath the woman's skirts. At first she was miserably cold. But she had a strong heart so her body began to warm the river around her and she felt strangely at home.

The woman thought of her daughter all of the time. She learned not to cry her tears while swimming near eddies above the deepest holes of the river. Although the biggest fish loved these dizzying currents, the woman knew she must not let herself slip in. She still feared the desire to stay below and not rise to the surface. Months before, she had accidentally fallen off a rock. She did not realize how far under the surface she had dropped because her tears, the size of ponds, were so heavy and the pull of the eddy so strong. The river rose rapidly above her. She opened her eyes, feeling very cold and when she looked up she could not see the surface. She also noticed that she was not greatly disturbed by this. However, far above she heard all those whom she loved screaming her name. The woman kicked her legs as hard and as fast as she could, and propelled herself out of the water onto their laps and into their arms. She was so relieved and grateful that they kept calling for her. Later, after she was warm and dry, she sat against the trunk of her favorite tree and watched the river become lost in its endless movement and beauty.

I

Twelve Days of Christmas

With each loss the trapdoor opens beneath our feet and we fall, feeling the terrible wind, gazing upward at a life now forever out of reach.

—Philip Simmons, *Learning to Fall*

1

Portrait of Melissa: Diving

Barefoot and with measured step, she moves silently toward the precipice. Just as her toes extend over the edge, she stops. I watch from a distance and don't breathe. There's nothing I can do but wait. My palms sweat. Suddenly she springs upward and somersaults forward twice before slicing into the water with arrow-shaped fingertips. I never know what will happen when her toes leave the plank. I'm not prepared for this but she is. Despite how precisely she executes the exquisite brain-body motion there is room for random error. Sometimes she walks to the end of the diving board, turning at the last minute so that her heels hang over the end. I think of the classic trust exercise in which an individual practices surrendering to others by falling backwards into their supportive arms. Melissa has no one to catch her in case her dive fails. There is no safety net. In the past I've seen her head miss the board by a few millimeters on the way down, a collective, "Ooh!" escaping the lips of the gathered crowd.

What will happen this time? I forget any discomfort from the heat and high humidity while holding my winter coat. Reaching for the heavens her body rises, arches backward, gracefully soaring. Descending, it realigns. *Splash.* A quiet waterworks from the surface of the pool: a successful dive. Force and gravity pull her under. She emerges looking like a wet seal. Gliding to the edge of the pool, she climbs the ladder in an effort to match wits once more with that lively plank.

Watching her, I see Melissa as a young woman practiced in the art of falling. Externally, she is a study in passion, focus, and coordination. I imagine her mind as a display of sizzling sparklers, as millions of neurons fire with each anticipated dive.

There was no way to know that this complex internal-external show would burn out at twenty-five, in little more time than it takes to blow out candles on a birthday cake. Neither could I know that I would experience my own fall, flailing into the darkness.

2

I Wasn't There

I wasn't there when flashing lights and sirens raced to my daughter's apartment on that early morning in December 2001. I don't remember if there was snow yet that year, but I think it was overcast. I wasn't a witness to her boyfriend Eric's attempt to help her breathe once he realized something was terribly wrong. I don't think they were even out of bed that morning when she started making unrecognizable sounds. They were probably still groggy with sleep. Doctors later told us that the cardiac arrest may have been preceded by a seizure. All I know are bits and pieces of information. And that I wasn't there.

Work is where I was, at the outpatient mental health program located in the same hospital where Melissa would soon arrive through the emergency doors several corridors away. I would find out where she was in about three hours. I can never decide which is more unnerving: to remember when life was normal or to remember believing that it was normal, when in fact it was not.

The morning for me was a typical Friday, proceeding according to schedule, until I got the phone call from John. Events before that moment are mostly forgotten. It is the details of what was happening in her apartment a few blocks away for which I'm starved. Even now, years later, I would listen with rapt attention to a minute-by-minute or second-by-second report if such a thing were available. Cardiac arrests take effect at warp speed. I have learned that it takes a mere three to four minutes before brain damage begins. Often I get stuck on that fact, going around and around. I suspect I am hoping to change the facts and thereby change the outcome.

I wasn't there when the EMTs arrived. What exactly did they see when they walked in the door of the apartment? What theories did they form about the crisis in front of them? What did they do first? I suppose they assessed her quickly. Later I was told they determined that her heart was in ventricular fibrillation. They shocked her twice, regulating her heart's rhythm. I wasn't there to ask questions or answer questions. Where was Eric? Was he in the bedroom watching, hugging himself in absolute terror? I wish I had thought to ask him. During all the commotion did Jezebel, Melissa's cat, hide in darkness under the living room couch, heart racing, eyes darting and ears reacting to each unfamiliar sound? She, of course, could not know that she would never again feel Melissa's hand stroking her back or scratching her head. Nor could she know she would never hear those endearing nicknames meant just for her.

I wasn't there when the EMTs left the apartment. They probably laid Melissa on a gurney covered with a blanket to protect against the December cold. I wonder what color the blanket was. My imagination provides only a black-and-white version of the picture. I wish I could talk to these people who worked to keep her alive. It's been a long time. I suppose they have forgotten her crisis by now. My secret agenda, kept perhaps even from myself, is that if the scene were vivid enough then I could imagine her alive again and could still hold her warm hand.

I wasn't there when the ambulance shrieked, demanding the road as it shot like a bullet back to the hospital. As my world was secretly detonating behind my back, mid-morning continued to find me calmly immersed in what I thought would be another predictable Friday. I felt happy remembering that John, Melissa, and I were going to a restaurant the next afternoon to have a special English tea, something only offered during the holidays. Any pleasure I was feeling was interrupted when my friend and colleague, Nancy, took a phone call from John. When she informed him that I was consulting with a psychiatrist about a client, John said, "This is urgent."

That morning John had breakfast with one of his closest friends, enjoying a leisurely start to this ordinary December Friday, before heading off to the University of Minnesota where he'd been a professor of political science for almost three decades. They probably caught up on a few personal issues and made "very savvy" predictions about trades affecting the next baseball season. Or they may have been discussing the state of the country given that the Twin Towers in New York City had disintegrated a mere three months earlier. Breakfast at their favorite neighborhood café probably left them warm and satisfied.

John arrived at work and got started with a busy day. He left his office for a meeting and didn't return until late morning. As he was about to go into another meeting he noticed a message on his answering machine. It was from a hospital social worker. It was a message that would change his world. When he returned the call, the social worker had gone to lunch. A doctor spoke to him instead. The doctor summarized what had happened and told John that Melissa had been intubated, i.e., a tube had been inserted into her windpipe to help her breathe. John remembers that although the doctor said he was sorry, his tone seemed emotionless. I wasn't there to see John's relaxed expression switch off as he tried to comprehend the implications of what he was hearing. I wasn't there to see his fear and frustration as he drove his car from the office toward the emergency room at the hospital in what must have felt like slow motion.

I wasn't there when my son, Brandon, answered the telephone and heard Eric's voice telling him that his sister was in the ER and he should come right away. Brandon and his wife, Megan, happened to be at home packing. They were getting ready to leave for Wisconsin where they planned to have an early Christmas celebration with Megan's family. I imagined them feeling scared and perplexed as they grabbed their coats on the way to the car.

That morning I ran quickly from my predictable life and professional world into the hospital's ER with hope that Melissa would soon recover. As hard as it was to believe later, I did not fully understand the seriousness of the situation. Melissa was young and, I thought, healthy. I told myself that her condition would be fixable. By the end of the day, medical reality had melted my illusions. I started to fall, grasping at the air that slipped through my fingers.

I was now part of Melissa's tragedy as it continued to unfold. I was Melissa's mother. I was finally in the right place and was always there.

Melissa was put on life support.

We would need life support as well, but didn't know it at the time. And so began the last twelve days of Melissa's life and ours as we knew it. Oh, how I would love to return to those first days when we still had hope that she could come back to us, when anoxia was only a word found in a medical dictionary, and when we still held the belief that modern medicine was much further advanced than it really was. In the strangest of ways the memories are almost sweet now, and I find that I want to gorge on them.

3

Crisis and Chaos

We once had a cat named Yilga. John named her after a minor character from The Gormenghast Trilogy (Mervyn Peake), which he was reading at the time. She was an ordinary gray tabby from the Humane Society. Except for her name, and the fact that she lived to be over nineteen-years-old, there was nothing outstanding about her. However, she had one quirk. She had a seven-second delay: when either of us called her, it took her to the count of seven to get up and move. John and I often looked at each other and wondered what could possibly be passing through her little brain during that recurrent lapse of seven seconds.

On December 14, 2001, when I heard John's voice urgently telling me to go to the Emergency Room, my brain seemed to pause like Yilga's. I was organized for a different set of activities. I had to stop and, for a few seconds, didn't know how to turn myself in another direction. So many thoughts flooded through my brain that I couldn't sort them out. It didn't take those around me long to tell me to "Go!"

Once my body and my brain were back in sync, I moved quickly to search for Melissa who was supposed to be in the ER. When I got there I was informed that she had been transferred to the ICU. As I headed for the elevator I ran into Megan and Brandon. Together we made our way to the unit and were told where we should wait for the doctor. The room seemed very light even though it had no windows.

John arrived and sat down beside me. The space of the room was quickly filled with our anxiety and confusion.

Soon, a doctor came in and helped give our minds something to focus on. He told us that the medical team was still trying to stabilize Melissa. The only information we were given was that Eric had awakened earlier in the morning to find her making a strange nasal sound and having no pulse. He had called 911 and tried CPR. When the medical team arrived they applied shocks twice. According to medical reports, while still in the apartment, Melissa had probably already displayed "decorticate posturing." This is a kind of abnormal posturing in which the body rigidly contorts causing the arms to bend inward toward the body. The wrists and fingers bend also and are held on the chest. This is considered one sign of severe brain damage. No one knew why the cardiac arrest had occurred or how long her brain had lacked oxygen. In terms of survival and level of functioning following a cardiac arrest, everything depends on the degree and length of time without oxygen. My questions about what had happened were put on hold.

After the meeting, we moved to the ICU waiting room. The top priority of Melissa's medical team was to keep her alive. Doctors updated us intermittently throughout the day.

As the day progressed a life-threatening medical event occurred. The treatment team determined that a "CVC (central venous catheter)/ arterial access" needed to be inserted. A catheter of this kind can serve a number of important functions, such as administering medication, monitoring, and taking blood draws. The insertion requires surgery and is commonly performed by an anesthesiologist. The treatment team repeatedly requested that a doctor be sent who could do this surgery. However, as the hours passed and no one came, the treatment team became very alarmed; Melissa's status was unstable and her life was in imminent danger. Out of complete frustration and in fear of further delays, the team realized that the only thing they could do was call a "Code Blue." When a "Code Blue" is broadcast throughout a hospital, all available medical staff literally run as fast as they can to a patient's room, prepared to do whatever is needed to save a life. Melissa had the surgery. Following the crisis, a nurse filed an "incident report" that stated Melissa had received "lack of necessary access and compromised care." Regardless of the language of hospital protocol, Melissa almost died twice that day.

The crises of the first day in the ER and ICU were essentially medical dramas performed behind curtains and closed doors. There was no active role for me, her mother, to perform. As I waited, my dread, impatience, and helplessness thundered inside me. John, Brandon, and Megan were nearby, yet they, too, were left alone to do battle with their own private terror.

During the first several hours of our vigil in the ICU, few people in our lives knew what had happened. At that time our support circle was only a small intimate gathering of family members. Collectively we maintained a laser-sharp focus, hoping to spot a doctor walking across the carpeted waiting room. We were desperate for any information about Melissa's condition and hopelessly vulnerable to any implied prognosis. At that point, it was only communication with the doctors that had the potential to provide us with any comfort. Yet without our small family huddled together, and a few close friends who stopped by off and on, our terror and dread would have been overwhelming.

Only at the end of the day were we able to see Melissa in her room for a short period of time. Although we felt reassured to see her calmly breathing with the help of the ventilator, we also felt dread knowing another crisis could break the spell at any moment.

John and I stayed the night in a small, dark room, which was attached to the larger ICU waiting area. My bed was a black leather recliner. I still wore my work clothes; I used my coat as a blanket. There were no bedtime rituals that night. Pajamas, slippers, and robes had no place; I might have to burst into consciousness, tearing into the stillness of the night to be at the bedside of my child who might be dead or dying. Watching the 10 p.m. news would have seemed like something I would do on another planet. My entire world was now based on news stemming from one story taking place in one room, on one unit, and in one hospital. Anything that interrupted the crisis at hand felt like an emotional violation. Terror ruled time, dragging John and me unwillingly through each minute.

4

Cautious Hope

It was only after the sun rose the next morning that we were informed the infamous angel of death had passed Melissa by. This was an unbelievable relief. I felt as though we were all lucky again. There was still hope. If her body was strong enough to survive the night, who could predict what this new day might bring? But soon the relief became an uneasy one. What I didn't yet know was that we had escaped nothing. Soon we would be required to make the most difficult decision of our lives. However, on this morning Melissa was alive. Hope reigned.

As a new day began, John and I continued to meet with doctors as they discussed the meaning of the most recent lab results. Nothing else mattered. The doctors used medical terminology that we really did not understand or have the ability to put into a meaningful context. At the time we wondered, how exactly does a cardiac arrest differ from a heart attack? Did Melissa have a heart condition that had gone undetected? What is anoxia (insufficient oxygen to the brain)? How does a coma induced by anoxia differ from one caused by a head injury? What is hypokalemia (low blood potassium)?

We were told that when Melissa arrived in the hospital, her potassium level was very low. Initially we didn't understand the full significance of this fact, or know how her level compared with the normal range. The doctors, from a clinical perspective, were trying to put together the pieces of what had happened to Melissa and at the same time assess whether they could help her. Low potassium is familiar to people in the medical community who work specifically with eating disorders. There are multiple causes for a low potassium blood level; however, purging behavior is a primary suspect, especially if there are no other apparent medical causes. So along with all the other questions we faced, we began to speculate that eating-disordered behaviors may have caused the very low potassium, which in turn caused the cardiac arrest. I felt as though I needed several mini-seminars ASAP.

There was no way to reconstruct Melissa's possible unhealthy behaviors during the recent past so that we could understand the reason for her low potassium level, which was 1.6 milliequivalent per liter when it was tested in the hospital. Anything lower than 3.5 milliequivalent is considered low. John and I felt perplexed: how could she have functioned if she was this seriously ill? Yet she had helped me decorate the Christmas tree two evenings before, had called us the night before looking for something to do and had stopped by Brandon's house to chat, also wondering if he was free to go out. In addition, the night prior to the cardiac arrest, Melissa had played chess with Eric. He said that she had played well. When asked, he said that he had noticed no purging.

My mind kept insisting that her cardiac arrest was not caused by the one obvious behavior that Brandon, Megan, and her caregivers theorized. How could she have had a cardiac arrest given that she had never been assessed or diagnosed by a mental health professional as having had an eating disorder. She had never been hospitalized nor had any previous close calls. Although I was focused solely on the present, I would discover that this yearning for absolute knowledge would haunt me for years to come.

The time between consultations with doctors was a space filled with high anxiety. We received basic information as it became available. However, because our brains were flooded with stress, we had trouble absorbing the information. All we wanted to hear were words, understood or not, telling us that our child would live and recover. We were starved for any exam or test result that would enlighten us about Melissa's condition and prognosis. Absolutely nothing else mattered. Doctors bearing test results equaled hope or no hope. The stakes were as high as they could go. So when sober-faced doctors quietly walked toward us in their white lab coats, IDs suspended from pockets, obedient stethoscopes curling around their necks, I held my breath. I wanted to scream, "Stay away unless you can lead us out of this hell. I cannot live if I lose my daughter." But I submitted out of desperation. I knew decisions that would follow from Melissa's prognosis and treatment would be ours to make and that we needed to be informed and realistic.

While the emotional and rational parts of me battled, doctors spontaneously arrived with updates. I knew they wouldn't stay long. The pressure built. I would tell myself, "Make sure to ask all of your questions now. You'll regret it if you don't... But what did s\he just say? What does that medical term mean?" It was stressful trying to know what to ask when I didn't know for sure what had been said. I had my pride. God forbid I should sound like an idiot in the presence of these medical professionals.

After a couple of days, a friend of ours who had medical training as a nurse brought us a 1998 article from *The Lancet*, a well-respected medical journal. The article, entitled "Evoked Potentials Not Just to Confirm Hopelessness in Anoxic Brain Injury," highlighted fundamental signs to look for in a comatose anoxia patient that indicated a better or worse prognosis. I left the task of reading it in detail and analyzing it to others who were familiar with data analysis. My brain was too scattered so I was grateful that others could support me in this way. Even though John and I didn't know precisely how to apply the information to Melissa's condition, the article was something concrete on which to focus as we waited.

With heads drawn together in concentration, we pored over the main points of the article. What was crucial were the specific ways Melissa's body was reacting as the hours in the coma accumulated. The article stated, "Fewer than 40% of patients in coma (those caused by lack of blood to the brain) for more than 12 hours make a meaningful recovery." But no one knew how long Melissa had been without adequate blood flow. Two variables that indicate poor prognosis by day three are "absent pupillary responses" and "absent motor response to pain." Except for a slight reactivity in her left eye, Melissa showed almost no reactivity. Each day that passed built a more impenetrable wall between Melissa and the world, between us and her.

In general, we learned that the number of hours in a coma was linked to the outcome. The shorter the coma the more likely the patient might recover without neurological damage. The longer the coma the more likely there would be severe damage. The first day inevitably pushed on to day two and then day three. At first we had measured time in terms of survival and physical stability. However, as progress was made toward those goals, and the coma remained, we wanted time to slow down. We felt as though we had capsized in the middle of a rapidly flowing river and were headed for a waterfall. The currents would determine our fate. Although we still had hope, our expectations for Melissa's recovery began to drop.

During those days in the ICU we scrutinized Melissa's every

movement searching for an indicator of good news. I learned things about the human body that I never wanted to know. One is that a person's body can stay alive as long as the brain stem, which controls basic functions such as breathing and blood circulation, is not damaged. Although the brain is protected by the skull, it remains incredibly vulnerable. Once damaged in particular ways, it will not restore its functioning no matter how much we weep.

I also learned that there are different kinds of comas, some resulting from head traumas and spine injuries, such as from a car accident or a fall. We've all read stories about people who wake up after days, weeks, and sometimes much longer, and still retain their personalities and often much of their ability to function. In some cases, with time and rehabilitation, new neurological connections can grow. Sometimes doctors will induce comas as a treatment for certain conditions.

I feel bitter realizing that medicine has advanced to the point of doctors inducing comas but not being able to pull a patient out of one. But when a coma results from lack of oxygen to the brain (anoxia), which only takes a few minutes, parts of the brain die, and if the damage is severe, under no circumstances can those parts be restored. A person in this kind of coma can actually "wake up," but not in the way most of us think. This "waking up" occurs without any self-awareness or awareness of the environment. In other words, the patient can't make sense of sensations or stimuli. When this neurological state goes unchanged, the individual may soon be diagnosed as being in a "persistent vegetative state."

One important thing I learned was how much more terrified I should have been in 2001 when I first heard the words, "cardiac arrest." Even now, my pulse races when I hear those two words.

After the first several days passed we began to develop a more realistic perspective about the seriousness of Melissa's condition. We stopped thinking about her returning to us as the person she had been. We knew that her brain had been injured, but the details were still unclear. Sometimes she moved a little, igniting cautious hope that perhaps she still had a chance to have a life. We began to fantasize a future with her even though it would be radically different from the past. We imagined her in a rehabilitation program with us actively assisting her in reaching a new potential. And so we continued to wait for her to wake up so we could get on with our work. We had no idea how off the mark we were.

5

Life Support Begins

As the news of Melissa's hospitalization spread to people who knew her and us, more and more of them moved gently toward us with worried, loving faces. They joined us in our current hangout, the family waiting area in the Intensive Care Unit. The kitchen nook became stocked with food as our new life supporters brought fruit, snacks, sandwiches, sweets, drinks, and home-cooked meals; nourishment for anyone who joined in our vigil. Although in my desperation I had little appetite, I felt nurtured, as well as sustained, by each person and any gift of food or drink that was placed on the countertop.

Each of them hugged us when they came and when they left. Having come from a loving family, but not one that hugged often, I was surprised by how quickly I began to welcome the comfort I felt when encircled within two human arms. Again and again this gesture of caring and concern was given. At the time, we did not know that a container for our emotional trauma was being molded. This invisible structure was fortified each time our life supporters provided us with their sustaining constancy. This dynamic container would hold us for years to come.

I continued to marvel at the number of people who stepped forward from our lives.

One day a nurse informed me that we needed to have fewer visitors at any given time because it was too noisy for other families in the waiting lounge. She also said that we needed to leave more space in the kitchen nook for others. I felt rather embarrassed given that I usually tried to be considerate of others. However, since I was almost completely absorbed in my own pain I was less aware of others. In addition, I was deeply grateful to each person who came to visit and didn't want to put limits on their support. My friend Nancy came to my rescue and helped manage this problem.

Melissa's friends from high school and college began to arrive. When I saw them walk in, I felt pangs of grief even though I still didn't know how our story would end. All I knew when I saw their familiar young faces was that Melissa should be with them, planning where to go out for dinner that evening in order to catch-up. Two of these friends had just flown in from Chicago. Melissa had known them since grade school. They had years of shared memories of sleepovers, biking, hiking, canoe trips, and hanging out with each other. Together they were truly joyful—loving each other like sisters. Now, as young women preparing for professional careers, their worlds had expanded. However, they quickly reunited around life events such as weddings and, obviously, crises. It was wonderful to see them. They were living proof that Melissa had had a rich life.

There was a small group of friends, usually arriving in a trio—Dan, Seth, and Wendy—who made frequent visits to the ICU. Seth, Wendy, and Melissa had lived together for a couple of years in a small house at college, which they had named the Smurf House because it was little and blue. Following graduation they all settled in the Twin Cities. They continued their close friendship, which then included Dan. Wendy was in medical school at that time, receiving training in neurology. She wore red-framed glasses, which seemed like an exclamation point to the optimism she expressed about Melissa's condition. And since, in the first few days, the prognosis was unknown, it was comforting to imagine a positive outcome. Seth, Dan, and Wendy emotionally helped us more than they could ever know. Each time they waited with us they brought a youthful spirit that helped to calm me, allowing me to immerse myself in this part of Melissa's previously rich world. I felt more hopeful. Maybe Melissa would come out of her coma and enjoy her life again with these and other loyal, loving friends.

In addition to Melissa's friends, John and I began to notice not only a changing cast of characters but also certain individuals quietly returning time after time, obviously spending most of their non-work, non-sleeping time with us. Joel was one such friend. I remember pausing to look around the waiting room and there he would be again, calmly and quietly waiting with us and for us; waiting for us to express a need or to talk while he listened understandingly. He knew about the pain of grief having lost a beloved wife some years earlier. At first I approached him as if he were sitting in my living room and I was asking him if he would like a glass of wine before dinner. Specifically, I usually started by asking him how he was doing or by launching into a medical update regarding Melissa's status even though there wasn't much to say and he wasn't asking for anything. I was trying to be social in an ordinary way, maybe even trying to take care of him, uncomfortable with the fact that he and others were there to support me. I remember when he let me know this by saying, "You don't have to take care of me. I'm fine. It's not about me. I'm completely fine just being here." You see, Joel helped me by being kind and direct.

I asked others as well, "How are you?" causing them to deflect the question very quickly. Eventually John pointed out the pattern of my behavior, and I stopped doing it. The problem was that at some point I had started to think of myself as "pathetic" and I hated it. You would think I could let myself off the hook since I was in the middle of a highly charged crisis. But how I typically saw myself and my life didn't fit with the new situation. I had trouble accepting the reality and tried to behave as though it weren't true. My unintended persona as the hostess of some macabre open house merely highlighted my struggle. I was automatically assuming a familiar role even though I was completely lost.

Psychologically my situation was forcing me to feel uncomfortable with the ways I usually defined myself in relationship to others and how I coped in general. I was usually quiet about any problem I had, relying on myself or my family to deal with it. However, I was so far removed from anything that I had previously faced in my life that my walls began to shake loose. It was impossible for me to take care of myself in private anymore. Everyone else understood that I was not expected to be alone in this crisis. They knew why they were with me even if they didn't always know what to do.

One of the things I did not know at the time was that after Joel's wife died, while he was in the early, raw part of his grief, he had life-support friends who invited him to spend time in their homes. Sometimes rather than wait for an invitation he asked them if he could come over. He told us that it was enough to just sit while others' lives went on around him. Another thing I learned from Joel was that one of the people who offered him a spot on her couch while she quietly sewed, who sensed his need to not be alone and who was able to sit close to his pain, was Lee, who later became his wife.

Lee and Joel complemented each other as they reached out to us. They were like a pair of weighted bookends that we could count on to remain stalwart, to not slide apart, ensuring that we remained upright when on our own we might have tipped to the side or spilled onto the floor. Yet they also flexed in their help, dancing the complicated moves and steps in the style of true grief supporters.

One of the first days in the hospital, Lee quietly handed me something. It had a smooth lavender cover, which turned out to be a journal. Lee was focused when I could not be. She was centered and calm when I was not. She softly suggested that I might find it useful to write down some things. After thanking her, I thought, "It's a good idea, but I really don't think I'll use it." I had never kept a journal before. After a week or so, I did start writing in it in an attempt to express my terrifying thoughts and feelings. I continued to do so for a few months, until gradually the time came when I didn't need to use it as often. But it was still there. Lee knew something I didn't know. I just hadn't caught up with it, emotionally.

6

Coma Continues

Each day in the ICU passed slowly with an unrelenting demand to answer the same questions. Would our sleeping princess ever awaken? Was she showing any signs at all of doing so? Our desperation rose. She was running out of time. Only doctors in white lab coats showed up; never a prince on a white steed. In spite of all the love, the desire to help and top-notch medical doctors and treatment, chances were that Melissa was not going to "live happily ever after."

After entering Melissa's room, I would gently caress her hand, her leg, sometimes her hair, frustrated that the ventilator tube kept me from getting close to her face, as I so wished to do. I wanted to press my cheek softly to hers or perhaps lay my head next to hers on the bed. But there were too many obstacles. The cool rigid aluminum railings also made it hard to get close. I understood the safety and health reasons for these imposed obstacles, but when it is your child in that bed you want to be as close as possible.

Holding Melissa's hand was the most comfortable human contact because, whether I was standing or sitting, I could easily slip mine into hers. Her hand, of course, did not fold around mine but it did not pull back either. It was the best she and I could do under the circumstances. I remember how the underside of her hand felt a little rough. Then I would remember how much she had used her hands throughout her life and in so many different ways. Sometimes, when my grandson Kieran puts his hand in mine I think of Melissa's because his hand also feels rough. He is an explorer of the world as well.

Eventually, I wanted to scream. I knew we needed a miracle. The signs of a "meaningful recovery" were overdue. The article that we had scrutinized intensely for three days was becoming irrelevant. My beautiful twenty-five-year-old daughter lay unresponsive in a coma with brain damage. This image did not fit into a future photo album. Yet there she lay; and there I was looking down upon her. Like most hospital patients, Melissa looked anything but elegant. A plastic tube connected to a ventilator pumped oxygen into her lungs. Some of her bottom teeth were loose as a result of biting down too hard on the tube. Her hospital gown, thin and faded, smelling of something that must have been disinfecting detergent, was wrapped loosely around her. So although she looked nothing like the star of an animated Disney tale, I felt like one of the forest animals who gathered around the glass-covered casket, powerless, keeping a desperate vigil, feeling frustrated and terrified beyond words.

Soon we started asking the nurses and doctors, "How will we know if Melissa is coming out of her coma?" "Oh, you'll know when she wakes up" was the response. Although this answer seemed pretty vague, even a little mysterious, it set off a spark of hope and gave us something to focus on. So far Melissa appeared as though she were in a chronic deep sleep.

As we awaited the longed-for miracle, Brandon and Megan visited her every day. They and her friends did everything possible to bring her personality to life since she was not able to do so for herself. They brought in her favorite CD mixes, set up photos of her in the hospital room, and brought in her favorite stuffed animal—Felix the Cat—which John and I bought her when she came down with chicken pox at the age of six. They talked to her, hoping that she could hear them.

Her boyfriend Eric, who had been with her from the very beginning in their apartment and had the grave responsibility of calling 911, also spent hours with her. As the days passed, he showed up looking more and more rumpled and exhausted. I can only imagine how he must have pleaded from the core of his being that she would wake up. All of these young adults were valiant in their efforts to preserve her personhood in spite of her persistent muteness. They also wanted to make sure that those who were caring for her did not forget that she had been a lively, walking, talking young woman prior to being rolled into this room on December 14.

7

Identity Crisis Begins

John and I found it unsettling to be experiencing ourselves and our lives as if part of some Shakespearean tragedy. Prior to this time we felt we had a pretty lucky, special, and maybe even protected life. We talked about it sometimes. It wasn't as though we hadn't lost loved ones. Both of our fathers had died in their seventies. One of John's sisters had died at the age of thirty-one, leaving four small children, and an older brother had died well before old age. In addition, we had experienced a mix of common difficulties and stressors as in the course of most families. However, we also had wonderful things happen to us. Some seemed to stem from our own hard work and effort; others due to good luck.

Both of us grew up in a moderately small town, in families of modest means. Our parents were proud of us when we did well in school, but there were clear limits as to what they could provide for us once we left the family. Because a public college education was affordable at that time to many students, we were both able to graduate from college and John immediately went on to graduate school. The experience of upward mobility probably contributed to an enhanced appreciation of many of the good things we experienced in our lives as adults.

A generation later, John and I felt very proud of our children and the paths they were taking in their lives. As many parents do, we took partial credit for their development because of the support we had given along the way, yet we knew they deserved the majority of the credit.

However, when random bad luck selected our child and our family in such a severe fashion that would forever change our lives, the image we had of ourselves as individuals, as parents and as a family no longer fit. Our previous selves began to crack open like dried seed pods in the wind of a winter's storm. And so, an identity crisis began to unfold, stretching out before us over a long period of time.

8

Neurological Consultant

Life support came in a variety of forms from a growing number of people. One in particular came to us unexpectedly. His support would be invaluable during the time we made our most difficult decision. A friend of ours contacted one of her colleagues who was a Minnesota neurologist and a national expert in the areas of coma and unconsciousness. Susan asked if we would like to contact him as an outside consultant. He had already agreed to talk with us due to her efforts. Our hope was plummeting fast as the days accumulated with no change in Melissa's state of consciousness. We jumped at this opportunity. We had no idea what his fee might be or exactly when we would meet him.

On the day of his arrival, our hopes for Melissa's awakening had been raised. A nurse, who had consistently cared for her, suddenly called us into her room and said, "Look at this." She called Melissa's name and her eyes slowly opened. I was ecstatic. Seeing those aquamarine eyes flecked with golden brown was the most beautiful sight I had seen in days. John was right, I thought, when he had repeatedly said, "She always was a fighter and she will survive." Hope began to rise again. We especially wanted to talk with the consulting neurologist about this good news when he arrived.

In contrast to our usual pattern as a couple, John seemed more optimistic about Melissa's prognosis, and I was more pessimistic. However, historically, even when he felt pessimistic about a difficult problem, he would work extremely hard to solve it and often did. I worried that if Melissa didn't make it, he would feel compelled to try in vain to change reality rather than accept it.

Now that Melissa's eyes had opened, it seemed as though this could be the new beginning for which we had been waiting. I felt that I should be very gentle with her, as with something just born. She had the look of an infant coming out of a nap yet still asleep. We watched her intently with smiles on our faces. I still wondered, "Is this how she is supposed to look when she awakens?" Because this was the first time we had seen Melissa's eyes since admission to the hospital, it was very dramatic. However, beyond that movement, Melissa did little else. Was that enough? Increased hope led to increased patience as we waited.

My mind involuntarily took a photo of those eyes that will last for the rest of my life. Looking into them reminded me of the awe expressed by the astronauts describing the "blue marble" from outer space. Melissa was waking up . . . or so we hoped.

Several hours later, Dr. Cranford, the consulting neurologist, walked into Melissa's room. We felt beyond lucky, and grateful to Susan, who knew him and helped us make this connection. We were also very fortunate to have him agree to see our daughter so quickly, especially given that it was the holiday season. He had been a front runner in clinically defining "persistent vegetative states" and was a widely recognized consultant involved with difficult cases nationally, including the extremely controversial Terri Schiavo case. That case triggered a national debate beginning in May 1998 when Schiavo's husband fought in court with her parents to allow her to die after fourteen years in a persistent vegetative state. Terri's parents stated that they believed their daughter was still aware. However, according to her EEG, her cerebrum no longer existed due to degeneration as a result of oxygen deprivation during her cardiac arrest. In the end, after a long battle, the court allowed the removal of all life support and Terri died on March 31, 2005.

I was alone in the room when Dr. Cranford entered. John, Brandon, and Megan had briefly stepped out. As a friend of mine who has a quirky sense of humor and had been brought up Catholic might have said, I felt like "genuflecting." I was afraid that I wouldn't be able to answer questions he might ask. Providing him with a succinct, off-the-top-of-my-head medical progress report seemed way beyond my capabilities. No polite superficialities or smiles were exchanged. My anxiety skyrocketed. He read the chart and asked me a few questions. It was clear that Dr. Cranford was here to do his job—consult and give his best medical opinions. Our job was to receive this information, combine it with the reports, test results, and talks we had had with the hospital's doctors and then use it to help Melissa in whatever way we could.

Finally the others returned to join me. We gathered in a semicircle around Melissa's bed. I was so scared by what I might hear that John asked if I wanted to wait outside in the hall while Dr. Cranford examined her. I did, but of course, I also wanted to be there. I stood semi-buffered, standing a little behind Brandon, as though that would really help me cope. The word *bravery* was irrelevant to the situation. It had to be endured. The next few minutes were crushing as we waited to hear what this man had to say.

His approach was concrete and straightforward. Neither his exam nor his communication was nuanced. He moved around Melissa's body looking for specific neurological responses. He did a series of common neurological tests for assessing someone in a coma. One of the last tests he did was to take out his car key and run it under her left foot. Melissa's toes curled up. Dr. Cranford said, "That is not a good sign." I never would have guessed. If only they had pointed down as they always had when she was doing gymnastics. We told him that she had opened her eyes earlier in the day; that she also seemed to respond to certain sounds. This doctor pulled no punches with us as he replied that about half of brain-damaged people eventually open their eyes. It signified absolutely nothing.

That statement alone bore a hole into me like a fist into the wall. He added that individuals in Melissa's situation may even turn their eyes in response to sounds, and it still does not mean conscious awakening in the way we had hoped, or awareness. Dr. Cranford explained that the intact brain stem was merely doing its job. The higher functioning of the brain was not involved.

It was all bad news. He finished his exam, answered our questions, and gave a brief summary of his professional opinion, which was that Melissa's prognosis was grim. He told us that he was involved in doing research in which MRIs are taken on patients such as Melissa. This diagnostic test was not usually given in circumstances like hers and would not have been performed at that time without his request. He asked for our permission to have this done. Hungry to understand as much as possible, we said yes.

Before Dr. Cranford left us that evening he gave us his phone number with an open invitation to call him any time we needed to. We had much to think about. We were extraordinarily grateful to him. Knowing we could talk to him directly and easily was a crucial source of support. We consulted with him by phone two or three more times when we needed to understand complicated issues and identify our options. Without his ongoing support we may have been unable to face the life-and-death decisions to come.

Within hours we would be required to make these very decisions. We tried to come to grips with the fact that the last time we had seen Melissa fully functioning, only a few days earlier, would be the final memories of her with cognitive awareness. How utterly remarkable it was to experience my child as having lost her personality, her very identity. She seemed like a lovely seashell on the beach, rolling with the waves, catching grains of sand and drops of salt water, only a silent echo of herself remaining.

9

Bad News

In the article, "Medical Aspects of the Persistent Vegetative State" published in 1994 in the *New England Journal of Medicine*, "vegetative state" is defined as "a clinical condition of complete unawareness of the self and the environment, accompanied by sleep-wake cycles, with either complete or partial preservation of hypothalamic and brain-stem autonomic functions . . . patients show no evidence of sustained, reproducible, purposeful, or voluntary behavioral responses to visual, auditory, tactile, or noxious stimuli . . . no evidence of language comprehension or expression . . bowel and bladder incontinence . . . and have variably preserved cranial-nerve and spinal reflexes."

Dr. Cranford ordered an MRI; he consulted with the hospital neurologists and reviewed Melissa's records, tests, and charts. Shortly thereafter, we would find out whether there was even a low probability that Melissa would come out of her coma and/or have a meaningful recovery.

As we waited for the test results, John and I were told that Melissa's teeth, which had loosened from biting down on the ventilator tube, needed to be repaired. The doctors were concerned that she might choke on them if they loosened further. We were also told that she needed to have a feeding tube inserted into her stomach. Melissa might also be sent to rehabilitation. I thought all of this sounded promising. We were told that feeding tubes can even be temporary—who knew! A longer-term treatment plan was forming. All her electrolytes were back to normal. In other words, physically she seemed to be in quite good shape except for major portions of her brain.

Then the MRI results returned. The hospital doctors and Dr. Cranford consulted. We were called to a meeting. The abridged conclusion of their words was that it was, once again, all bad news.

10

Terror

At that moment something primal awoke, threatened. Blood surged, pumped by terror. Something against nature was happening. Freedom taken for granted was now destroyed. With pupils dilated, eyes darted, scanning the landscape. Hackled feathers, which moments before had lain smooth and quiet, sprang up. It was too late to stop. A great agitation had begun, with pacing and running, which went nowhere. What had seemed birdlike, began to howl. To this day, the creature goes unnamed, but it is recognizable to all who have been held hostage, caged by grief.

11

Decision: Life or Death

The doctors concurred that the worst imagined scenario had happened. There was massive, widespread brain damage. Within minutes any cautious hope vanished, throwing us headlong into foreign territory. What exactly was the enemy we faced? What should we do next? What options, if any, did we have? Melissa's nemesis, after sadistically holding her in its crosshairs for eight days, had finally pulled the trigger. Once again, my brain seemed to pause in the presence of the imminent and profound decisions we had to make.

Suddenly, the hospital system switched course and readied itself to move Melissa out of the ICU. As we tried to catch our breath we wondered what that meant for her and for us. What does one do with a comatose twenty-five-year-old daughter—consider a nursing home? Again we grabbed for the life-support line thrown by Dr. Cranford. It was critical, at that decision point, that he was an expert in ethics and neurology. John found his phone number and called him. The two of them talked about the medical, legal, and ethical issues involved in our situation and identified options to consider. The rest of us sat nearby, hearts pounding in quiet dread, waiting to hear John's full report. I was appreciative that he was willing and able to be the family's spokesperson. At the same time, I knew his stress level must have been unbelievably high as he tried to listen, make sense of new and complex information, and then help the rest of us understand.

The first decision our small inner circle had to make was whether to withdraw the ventilator tube. The expectation was that once this breathing support was completely removed Melissa might die very soon, perhaps even that night. John and I, Brandon, Megan, John's sister Maggie and her husband Mike, as well as Eric gathered in a conference room where our focus was on the question, "What would Melissa want us to do for her under these circumstances?" The primary complicating factor was whether there was any chance that Melissa could actually gain real awareness. If the answer to that question was negative—and that seemed to be the answer—it was clear to me what Melissa would want and that was what I wanted for her. But in order to answer that question we had to rely on medical reports and doctors' opinions, and the answer would still be based on probabilities. So even though Melissa's outcome seemed obvious, I knew all of us had to be satisfied that we were making the best decision possible.

Although we were respectful of one another, stress wore us down. At times annoyance and frustration were expressed. Some wanted to make decisions faster than others, probably out of their own need to end the torturous process, which could have no positive outcome. Others had questions and wanted to make sure that all of the information we had received was absolutely accurate and that we understood its implications. I was horrified at the thought of making the wrong decision. At the same time, I wondered whether death was much different from a life controlled exclusively by a brain stem. We slowed down our decision-making process as we weighed these life-and-death questions.

After John's consultation with Dr. Cranford, and more discussion and clarification among ourselves, we were able to come to a consensus. We made the excruciatingly painful decision to have the ventilator tube removed. We were all certain that Melissa would have hated to be kept alive by artificial means only to slip into a vegetative state, in a nursing home, day after day, perhaps year after year with no awareness and no control.

That night after the tube had been removed, a male nurse in familiar blue hospital scrubs with a warm demeanor and military fitness came to the conference room where we had made the final decision. He said that he would prepare her so we could see her to say our good-byes. When we entered her room the light was dim. The nurse had brushed her hair into a pony tail. Her skin softly glowed, reflecting the light.

Felix the Cat was tucked under her arm. She looked lovely and very alive in the warmly lit evening. As we stood around the bed gazing down upon her, we each expressed our good-byes. In spite of the closeness of being together, I felt utterly alone, cocooned in sorrow.

Melissa surprised us. She did not die that night.

In 2002, the *Healthcare Ethics Committee Forum: An Interprofessional Journal on Healthcare Institutions' Ethical and Legal Issues* published an article entitled "Hospital Policy on Terminal Sedation and Euthanasia." Dr. Ronald Cranford, our neurological consultant, and Dr. Raymond Gensinger defined four categories of medical care that apply "when the goal of curing a patient or prolonging life is no longer held." They are: "foregoing medical treatment, palliative care, physician assisted suicide, and euthanasia." We decided on the option referred to as "terminal sedation," which is a kind of "aggressive palliative care." A patient receiving terminal sedation is given sedating medications but no nutrition or hydration. In simple words, the goal is to keep the patient comfortable through the dying process.

The hospital offered to move Melissa to a room on the oncology unit until she died. My grief level already seemed to be at its peak; therefore, this move provided some relief. We accepted the offer with gratitude. I had been terrified that the hospital would discharge her to us to take home. I felt as though I did not have the emotional strength it would take to watch her gradually die over the course of several days. I think death might have traumatized me in such an emotionally intimate and enclosed space. My heart throbs with terror even now as I imagine what it might have been like.

Years later I reflected on our decision process. None of us was medically trained. We were vulnerable to and dependent on a medical system that seemed like a giant octopus with far-reaching tentacles. We needed to trust the medical experts who had cared for and assessed Melissa and at the same time we needed to advocate for her. We were expected to absorb complex medical information, accept it on faith, yet be assertive with our questions, digest it all, draw the best conclusion, and then make a life-and-death decision based on the law and medical ethics. We were extremely grateful for all the help we received from within the hospital setting and from our consulting neurologist. I can tell you that when the really big questions regarding "end-of-life decisions" are asked, when a doctor looks directly at you, waiting for the "final answer," and you want to say, "Let me out of here I can't do this," that will not be an option. It will be up to you, the non-expert, to decide—even though you are bursting with grief and stress. Your feelings may need to be put aside temporarily as you consider what your loved one might have wanted. For any of you who have been in this kind of position—or have supported someone who was—it is important to know that you have been forced into an impossible situation. Time pushed you onstage demanding a performance before you were ready. It is no wonder doubts may linger afterwards. The best to hope for is that you will gradually become at peace with your decision over time.

12

Final Days

Thus began the longest journey—the four final days of Melissa's life. The medical conclusion was that Melissa's brain damage was so massive and widespread that gradually these areas of the brain would disappear. As long as her brain stem functioned, allowing her heart to beat and her lungs to breathe, she would be, physically speaking, alive. She would be unable to make sense of stimuli in her environment and, as a result, her body was at risk of becoming highly agitated. There was no need for treatment—only comfort care. Without food or water, death would prevail. How many days that would be, no one could tell us, but it would happen.

I felt a sickening dread, terror, and grief as I waited. This was a learning experience I never wanted to have, yet I later came to understand it is a decision people make every day on behalf of their loved ones. It felt like a kind of horror show in which I was forced to play a part. What a change from the previous days when an edgy hope permeated the bustle and intensity of the best equipment and medical care in the ICU!

The Oncology Unit was a quiet place, especially a few days before the Christmas holidays. Melissa was given a room at the end of a hallway, which meant she was farther away from us than she had been previously. Her medical status within the hospital had changed dramatically. She had become a patient in the process of dying. There was little monitoring equipment in her room. Fewer doctors and nurses attended to her or reported to us. There was no need. Though her body continued to breathe, she seemed to have become a shell of herself. I felt as though I was trapped in a living wake; attending a reviewal with a warm body.

We knew Melissa would never be able to come back to us. Yet our decision to allow her to physically die left us feeling frantic. We were assured she was given what she needed to be relaxed and comfortable. But the assurance did not quench the desperate desire to save her. Brandon, in his anguish, fought urges to stop the process. He imagined driving to the hospital in the middle of the night to give his sister food and water. I understood and my heart broke for him, and for her. Rationally, we all knew that the alternative decision would have been to allow Melissa to experience her environment for the rest of her life with no ability to make sense of it. In addition we knew that her body would stiffen, contort, atrophy, her hands would curl into hooks. And, no matter how much we loved her or how much care she received, her brain, the same one that had flashed with bright colors as she performed complicated, floor routines in gymnastics and did double twists off the diving board, would never be able to function in any capacity on its own again.

Although appearing calm as I waited, the engines of my body roared. Emotionally I was in overdrive fueled by fear, sadness, and anxiety. I spent most of my time in the waiting room with small couches and a TV that I hoped no one would turn on. Other families came and went. Our visitors came and went, fewer than when Melissa was in the ICU. This final holding area had no kitchen nook filled with food, snacks, or drinks. It had no large aquarium with interesting fish that at times had mesmerized me. This room had one function: it was a place to sit and wait. I had no need of a clock or a watch. Time was no longer measured in minutes or hours. Rather, it was measured by Melissa's breath. Like a gentle breeze flowing in and out, her breath at some random moment would stop, bringing her life to an end.

My needs were minimal. I sat. I stared at nothing. I talked occasionally with my family members, a doctor or nurse and a few visitors. Intermittently, I took the dreaded walk down the hall to see my dying daughter, kiss her forehead, remembering the nurse's instruction not to say or do anything that might cause agitation. This was because Melissa's brainstem was still intact. It did not require higher levels of brain functioning to react automatically to external stimulation, especially touch. In other words, she would feel it but not understand what was happening. If her body started having serious involuntary movements the only hope of managing them was by administering heavy doses of medications. So, even though there was not a ventilator tube getting between us, there was an invisible barrier that kept me at a distance.

After a brief visit, I would walk back down the hallway, returning to my chair until the next time.

Although we had fewer visitors we were pleasantly surprised several times when unexpected ones arrived. One instance was when Melissa's friend Alice and her family showed up. Their history with Melissa went back to the seventh grade. We had many warm memories of Alice and Melissa together. We remembered the ecstatic day Melissa turned sixteen-years-old and passed her driving test. She insisted that she be allowed to drive across town to Alice's house. She did get permission after a full parental discussion—something she always hated—and a firm promise that she would take city streets rather than the freeway.

Another day, just after our friend Nancy had brought us chicken soup, Melissa's high school boyfriend came to visit. We had not talked to Dan for several years. He said he had recently been told that Melissa was in the hospital. We were stunned at how he had grown into a man from the high school kid we had known. He was now training to be a doctor. This was a bittersweet visit we knew we would prize forever. His visit reminded us of how much Melissa had cared about him and how much we had loved him too.

I have one, and only one memory of being ironically amused during this living wake. A close colleague and friend of John's, Dan, stopped by to visit us on Christmas Day. I was impressed that he had left his own two young daughters and his wife to spend time with us in our wretched state. There was no doubt that his visit to see us reflected how authentically he lived out his values.

During our conversation, I told him that a chaplain on the Intensive Care Unit had forewarned us that our grief would probably intensify two months after Melissa died. Dan suggested that I put that on the calendar just to remind myself. What brought a smile to my face was to think that the grief I felt could actually get worse. I felt as though I had fallen through a threshold of misery and grief that could no longer register "better or worse."

Each visit to Melissa's room was excruciatingly painful. Each hour she stepped closer to death, we were reminded of the consequences of our decision. As Melissa's mother and father, we had to live with the knowledge that we had made a decision that would bring about her death. We believed we were doing the right thing and what Melissa would have wanted. Ethics and the law were in support of our choice. However, the result of the decision got in the way of wanting to be with her. A shift had taken place. I no longer felt as though I was spending time with my daughter—it was more like coming into the presence of death itself; one that I had caused. I felt tied in an impossible knot.

As we waited we asked ourselves the same questions over and over. "Are we sure of the prognosis?" "What is it based on?" "Do all the doctors agree?" "What are those main predictive factors again?" "What if someone read the wrong MRI and mixed up reports?" And on and on our minds circled even though we had reviewed the answers, discussed and arrived at a consensus multiple times with our inner circle of life support, doctors, and primary family members.

Intermittently, especially on December 24th and 25th, I imagined how people that we knew were gathered with their families—laughing, feasting perhaps, and feeling good just being together. All of these feelings were absent for me. For those close to us, I felt apologetic that our tragedy would be dulling the pleasure of their celebrations. Later, I realized how off my thinking was. I was still trying to function as though I was a child being told: "Don't draw attention to yourself"; "Don't bother anyone." Of course, our situation was deeply affecting those who cared about Melissa and us. That was exactly as it should have been. I wasn't practiced in accepting that one's priorities, plans, and feelings must change quickly when something horrendous has happened. I also wasn't practiced in being part of the focus of such attention.

As Melissa's life continued to fade, our lives seemed destined to be over as well. Imprisoned by the hopelessness of present events, I began to believe that the future would be forever blank: colorless, directionless, and joyless. We were like sheep, blinded in a downpour, floundering in mud on an eroded hillside. Disoriented and in danger, we needed a shepherd. We needed to hear whistles in the distance and barks of a sheep dog vigorously encircling, orienting us, and creating an invisible shield, while insisting that we climb to safety. Without being asked, our life support remained constant. They held on to us and we let them.

The horror of death expressed itself quietly, measured by Melissa's slowing inhales and exhales. I learned that approaching death does not have to be filled with moans or cries, or thrashing about. I learned that death can be desired, not an event from which to escape. As a mother I felt guilty. I told myself that I should be sitting with my child until her last breath, holding her hand. But I felt too much horror. I told myself Melissa would understand.

John and I moved through the days, winding in and out of rooms, sitting down, standing up, being hugged, listening to doctors, asking questions, almost completely confined to the present. Our eyes shut out the future, except as it related to Melissa. We were suspended as though we had all the time in the world. We were so preoccupied with the dark present that we didn't prepare for the ending.

13

The Spirit of Death

I picked up my pace as I made my way down the hall. As I approached the room where she lay, my steps slowed. I did not want to enter. Crossing the threshold, something caught my eye. I noticed how dark it was in the corner opposite Melissa. A shadow, much taller than me, seemed to be standing there immobile. Was I seeing things? Maybe, yet I knew that creatures who do not want to reveal themselves could remain motionless a lot longer than I could. Trying to make sense of what it might have been, I avoided looking at what lay on the bed. The longer I stared, the more the shadow seemed to take the form of a long black wing. Was there some kind of strange bird in this room of death?! I took one step closer, which confirmed it was indeed a wing with sleek, slightly curved feathers, each one tightly folded upon the other. It alarmed me that I could see no head. Transfixed, I could not move. How could I be expected to attend to my daughter's body while this huge being stood in the shadows? What was it going to do? Would it start to move when I wasn't looking, suddenly, slowly? As I finally turned to move toward the bed, it revealed a neck with something on top of it. Automatically I bowed my head. I couldn't look. For several long aching minutes, I was aware of each feather of its wing unfolding, eventually hovering over John, Brandon, Megan, and me like a huge black hood. I knew we were at its mercy. There was no protection here in this room. There would be no way out or way back home. This would be a moment of submission.

We were immobilized prey, stripped of all pride, our spirits filleted in order to feed that predatory creature. With no will of my own, I fell into the chasm of my fate, leaving behind this desperate distraction of my imagination.

I turned and walked to the head of the bed to give my precious child one last kiss on her forehead.

What kind of mother was I? I should have sat down on the bed and held her in my arms. Isn't that what mothers are supposed to do immediately after the death of their child? But I didn't want to. I was afraid. Melissa's eyes could no longer search for the sunlight. Her lips had no spirited thoughts to express or smile to give. Her once-active body lay as still as a stone on a rocky shore. My entire being knew I was now in the presence of death, not my daughter.

There are many unnerving images I can tolerate with the buffer of a television set or a movie screen. But in that room there was no emotional protection. I could not imagine what it was like for Brandon or Megan to see her in death, yet I knew there was nothing I could do to make it easier for them. It was a shared family experience, yet the reality was that we were four individuals completely alone in our own grief.

The sun had burnt out. Death reigned. Melissa's mouth with broken teeth was open. Her once beautiful eyes that we had prayed would open would not shut. I could see how the blood, which had stopped circulating, had pooled in the veins of her arms.

I think it would have helped all of us if she had been made to look a little more like her living self. Thomas Lynch, a poet, writer, and undertaker, referred to shutting the deceased's eyes and mouth in his book, *The Undertaking*, as "setting the features." Maybe that wasn't possible immediately after someone died in a hospital setting. I didn't know. This was an experience for which I was unprepared. I was grateful to have the one mental snapshot from the night in the ICU, several days before, when the ventilator was removed and we thought Melissa might die. The nurse had groomed her to look very much the way she had been in life. Of course, she was still alive then.

John and I had not attended church for a few years. Consequently, as I stood in Melissa's room minutes after she died I was at a loss as to what to do. I felt that I needed to hear words of a spiritual nature from someone who could join us in our overwhelming sorrow. However, we had no pastor to call and the chaplain with whom we had previously talked was not in the hospital that day. Falling back on the only thing I knew from my childhood, I requested that another chaplain come to us in Melissa's room and say whatever seemed appropriate. Later, it was hard to believe that we had not considered ahead of time what we would need and made preparations for it. Consequently, the hospital chaplain who joined us at Melissa's bedside and prayed with us had previously never met us or our dead child. However, I knew that I could not leave that room without a simple and fitting ritual that included words of transcendence.

A few minutes later the young nurse who had provided consistent care to Melissa led us to a small consultation room. She gave us Melissa's few remaining personal items as we signed the necessary papers. She was exactly Melissa's age and had graduated from a different college in the same small town. During the final four days I was frequently reminded of what a young life launched into a new career looked like and how Melissa was deprived of that experience. I felt cheated on her behalf. I also wondered what it was like for that nurse to be caring for a young woman her own age whose future was ending.

I remember when the nurse told me that she had gently touched Melissa's cheek and how Melissa seemed to like the feel of that touch. When I heard this I wanted to weep. I remembered when my little daughter found comfort in her yellow blanket with the satin binding and how she held this softness to her cheek while sucking her thumb. It was a reminder that emotional triggers would be lying in wait for me anywhere and anytime.

Other than those few final acts, the rest of the memories of that moment escape me. Only an autopsy remained to be done. Although there was some sense that a tremendous ordeal was over, emptiness and grief permeated everything as reminders that we had only experienced the prologue to this story. The vigil was over. Melissa had died on the twelfth day. Involuntarily, we continued our descent.

II

Grief

When we try to comfort others, most of us choose our words carefully, believing it's what we say: the wisdom, the insight that consoles. In my experience, this is not true. Grief occurs in the body as much as in the mind. Every cell is heavy with it, and neither words nor ideas relieve that weight. If anything comforts, it is the sounds themselves, the murmurings, the rhythms, the lilt of language so familiar it penetrates.

—Barbara McCauley, *Small Mercies*

14

Portrait of Melissa: Gymnastics

Running, she mounts the suede-covered beam in a test of balance and strength. At this moment all her attention is on a narrow surface, four inches wide and sixteen feet long. I watch, viewing the scene with admiration and dread, wanting it to be over as quickly as possible. But this is a timed event. I will not be granted my wish. I wonder if she will be able to go through her entire routine without a fall. Conversely, Melissa embraces the beam's challenge, attempting to woo it with difficult acrobatics and graceful movement. Her toes always point downward whether she is walking along the balance beam or holding it steady with her arms while she curves her legs overhead. Her hands also remain poised as the rest of her body goes through her routine on the four-inch strip. Like a vine deciding where to attach, she moves fluidly. Wearing the high school team's blue leotard with white gymnastic shoes molded to her feet, all eyes are upon her—just her.

I sit with others in a sea of silence holding my breath. She knows, and all who watch know, that if her balance is interrupted and she falls onto the mat it will jar both her body and her confidence. However, she also knows that whether she remains balanced or falls, her routine must be completed with the best poise and skill she can muster. If she lands on the mat, she will have exactly ten seconds to remount. Stopping for tears of frustration is not acceptable, and tears use up precious time. The mind must snap the emotions to attention, in order to finish the job.

Once the routine ends, she dismounts and waits for her final score to be announced. Suspense builds as the judges bend over their score cards.

Once again Melissa has chosen to face that taut, unforgiving beam with passion and palpable focus. And, one more time, I am awed by the physical and mental strengths that flow through her.

Melissa loved gymnastics and once declared, "Gymnastics is my life." She was passionate about it. She subscribed to *International Gymnast*, which featured articles and photographs of the best gymnasts from around the world. Numerous examples of the stars performing "perfect 10" moves hung from every wall in her bedroom.

Since her death I have repeatedly fallen into lapses of focus and despair. I have frequently succumbed to the urge to lie where I have landed and stay there. Melissa, however, has inspired me to get back up with renewed determination to take responsibility for my grief and my life. Through her example she has reminded me of a fundamental gymnastics rule—that the routine must be completed even if I fall.

15

Misplaced

Melissa did not like funerals. We knew she would choose not to have one for herself. We made the decision that cremation would be the best choice and found ourselves in new territory given that we had never been involved in arranging one. Fortunately, our friend Joel offered to help us make the first contact with the Cremation Society. Just as Melissa had introduced us to so many new experiences during her life, through her death, she introduced us to cremation.

Usually the transition from the hospital to the place of cremation is simple. First the family informs the hospital that they want their deceased loved one taken to a designated place. Then the deceased is picked up from the hospital after the autopsy, if one has been performed. The family meets with the cremation establishment, signs authorization papers, makes specific choices about the remains, and picks them up when they are ready.

When the Cremation Society arrived at the hospital, however, Melissa's body was nowhere to be found. Not only that, but the autopsy had yet to be performed. We were informed about all of this when the Cremation Society called us at home. They said it was urgent they receive the body that day, or everything would have to wait until the following Tuesday because of the upcoming New Year's Day holiday.

After hanging up the phone John and I were suddenly thrust into a crisis mode.

The image of my Melissa misplaced in the refrigerated stainless steel world of a hospital morgue a day after Christmas made me very, very sad. It angered me, as well. As a bereaved parent I felt as though my daughter's body was being dishonored. How could a hospital lose something so precious to me!!

As we sat at our dining room table trying to figure out what to do next, the phone rang again. This time it was a person from the organ donor organization. They couldn't have called at a worse time. I was raw with grief, shocked and sickened that my child was missing, and frantic to find her as quickly as possible. The person on the other end of the line had noble business to conduct, yet in my overwhelmed state of mind they seemed like a probing alien. I hung up on them a moment later, and I did so without regret.

Several days earlier, representatives from the donor organization had met with us in the hospital. At the time we weren't sure if it was a routine visit or if someone had contacted them. We later learned that a member of our group had done so. This contributed to our confusion. I remember little of that conversation. We may even have agreed to it. I just remember feeling as though the donor organization representatives were intruders—an irritant I didn't want to deal with. At that time my daughter was still alive. I was disoriented and distracted, trying to assess complex information about prognosis.

Looking back, I wish that this decision had been easier to sort out. I gained tremendous appreciation for the courage it takes for parents to deal with this choice under the saddest of circumstances. To discuss with a stranger the removal of parts of one's child who still breathes, but will die soon, is about as raw as it gets. I know Melissa would have wanted to be a donor. I'm sorry I deprived her of that privilege.

Through this experience of Melissa's body being lost, I learned how important it is to the bereaved that the body of their loved one be treated with dignity and respect. Again, Thomas Lynch writes, "The bodies of the newly dead are not debris nor remnant, nor are they entirely icon or essence. They are, rather, changelings, incubates, hatchlings of a new reality that bear our names and dates, our image and likenesses, as surely in the eyes and ears of our children and grandchildren as did word of our birth in the ears of our parents and their parents. It is wise to treat such new things tenderly, carefully, with honor."

In the end Melissa's body was found. The hospital hurried to get the autopsy done and her body was transferred to the Cremation Society within the needed time frame.

We felt so strongly about this misplacement that some weeks later, in order to give voice to our feelings, we arranged to meet with the head nurse from the oncology department. We asked her what had happened. She was professional and warm as she told us that because she had not been working on the day Melissa died, she could not clear up the entire mystery. She did inform us that some kind of communication mistake had been made, i.e., an internal paper had not been signed. Our questions were not completely satisfied, but we felt better because she had treated us respectfully and without defensiveness. It was the kind of interaction—given our intense need to understand and our raw emotions—that could have led to a very negative escalation. We gradually accepted that, however Melissa got misplaced, it was a minor chapter in the story of her death and our grief.

Upon arriving at the Cremation Society to pick up our Melissa's ashes, we were treated professionally, respectfully, and sensitively. John and I signed the authorization papers and asked that the ashes be divided into five parts. Megan or Brandon remembered that Melissa had once said she had a "variety pak" approach to life, bringing to mind the child-size cereal boxes that had delighted her. We intended to scatter her ashes in four places Melissa had especially loved and keep one-fifth for ourselves. We were taken to a room where many different urn designs were on display. I learned that there was a size, shape, and cost to fit any family's needs. A small green marble urn seemed to be right for us.

Once out of the hospital setting, I had more time to reflect on the various kinds of life support that were so crucial during the twelve days of our crisis. The full circle of our friends and family who gathered around us could not have done more. The many doctors, our neurological consultant, nurses, and other medical staff were competent, kind, and supportive.

A chaplain on the ICU was frequently available to us. Before he left for a holiday break, he informed us of his schedule and helped orient us to the Oncology Unit. I appreciated his help in preparing us for this major transition to a new environment, new staff, and the overwhelming emotional demands of observing our daughter die over a period of unknown days.

I began to think about the one source of support that seemed to be missing; in an ideal world, there would have been a person from the hospital setting serving as a liaison between the medical staff and us in order to explain medical terms and procedures, have an understanding of how lost a parent in our situation might be feeling, and to talk about the death process in a comforting way—and perhaps to be with us at the time of death if that was desired. We received some of this, yet needed so much more.

16

Remembrance Service

If it sounds as though we were unprepared for the end, we were. In fact, we were at sea for all stages of the experience. Our daughter was not supposed to die at age twenty-five. She was supposed to bury us. Now we found ourselves trying to guess what kind of service she would want us to plan for her. Would it be a funeral, a memorial service, a "celebration of life"? I helped plan my father's funeral and have attended many others, but these experiences didn't help much. All the traditional rituals had been thrown to the wind.

I began to think that an intimate family service was needed, followed by some sort of celebration of life event for those not in the immediate family. I wanted to drown in my grief and, except for family, keep others at a distance. On top of my grief, I privately carried a heavy layer of shame. Since I am a psychologist, and Melissa probably died as a result of some aspect of disordered eating, I felt acutely miserable and unworthy in front of others. John and I shared the view at that time that we should have intervened somehow so Melissa wouldn't have died. Sins of omission in one's mind can be just as damning as those of commission.

My mind felt fragmented when I considered the service. Planning and decision-making seemed overwhelming. I knew I needed help and direction. I didn't know how to take my deepest personal loss and grieve with others present. My lack of understanding about what others might need spoke to my own distorted sensibilities at the time. It was as if I wanted to claim all the grieving for myself and family, make it simple and do it in private; and only allow others to attend a "celebration of life" with storytelling and metaphorical clowns, balloons, and party hats. After opening up more with others during the previous few weeks in the hospital, I was retreating into my old habits. Fortunately, I was not allowed to get away with it.

The minister with whom we met at Unity Unitarian church will always have my deepest gratitude. John and I chose this church because it was where Melissa had gone through the "Coming of Age" program when she was fourteen-years-old. She had liked this church. She had friends there and had chosen one of her friend's mothers to be a mentor as she went through the "Coming of Age" program. When we met with Rob, one of the ministers, he set me straight almost immediately when I articulated my ideas for the service. He was very clear that everyone who knew and cared about Melissa needed an opportunity to grieve. A memorial service was one very important way to allow this. My idea of only the immediate family gathering to memorialize her was depriving others of honoring Melissa and grieving for her. Inviting others to only tell stories into a microphone was too limiting and distancing. He was so right.

I insisted, though, that a microphone be set up so that after the service anyone who wanted to tell a story or say something could do so. A few people used it to say a few kind words about Melissa. Friends did not get up to tell tales of joint escapades during high school or college. No one talked about memories of her as a child. Everyone was grieving. She had only left us several days before. In fact, every one of us was struggling to find words to articulate what had happened and what we were feeling. What had I been thinking?

It took nearly five years before a specific memory of Melissa amused me again and even then it was followed by a protective tightening in my chest. Thomas Lynch writes, "You know the part where everybody is always saying that you should have a party now? How the dead guy always insisted he wanted everyone to have a good time and toss a few back and laugh and be happy? I'm not one of them. I think the old teacher is right about this one. There is a time to dance. And it just may be this isn't one of them. The dead can't tell the living what to feel."

In the end, the service that we, with the help of many others, put together could not have honored Melissa more. The church bells tolled twenty-five times. Three friends gave thoughts of Remembrance. One included a story of how Melissa had once rescued an endangered baby sea turtle, which minutes later was snatched up by a swooping gull. We were told that her friends would ask her to tell this story over and over. The harpist played a heartbreaking arrangement of "Family" as we sat in the front pew, held hands, and wept. Afterwards in the reception line I was hugged many times, sometimes I smiled, chatted briefly with each person, felt the bitter sweetness with each of Melissa's friends, past and present, never wanting them to leave. I was hugged by a cousin whose face reflected the pain I felt and never said a word because there was no need. Fathers who had young adult daughters continued to weep into their handkerchiefs as they walked through the line. Dr. Cranford and his wife also surprised me with their attendance and hugs.

The food, laid out on long rectangular tables with white tablecloths, was catered by a friend who owned a local restaurant. This also made the event more personal and fit with Melissa's experience of growing up in the wider neighborhood. A group made up of her friends, Brandon and Megan, and our friend Lee had sorted through a stack of favorite photographs for framed foam boards. This display introduced her to people who did not know her directly and allowed those who did to remember her at all ages and stages. It turned out to be a celebration of Melissa's life after all, just different from what I had imagined. The only objection Melissa might have had was that all of the attention was on her. In that way, she would have been like her mother.

17

A Dark New World

It is often said when people die that they are "finally at peace." If only that applied to those left behind. I, too, wanted to be at peace and to rest, but there was much unexpected work ahead. There were changes and dilemmas to be confronted, which were made more complicated because Melissa's death had been unexpected and sudden. In *How To Go On Living When Someone You Love Dies,* Therese Rando writes about the sudden death of a loved one, "The loss is so disruptive that recovery almost always is complicated. This is because the adaptive capacities are so severely assaulted and the ability to cope is so critically injured that functioning is seriously impaired. Grievers are overwhelmed."

In January of 2002 I looked around and found myself in a dark new world. I didn't understand where I was or the rules that governed it. Yet I was forced to live in it. I felt like a prisoner, knowing that there was no escape. I felt fragmented, as though I didn't know who I was anymore. I felt different from other people except for a few who had also experienced major losses. The future seemed nonexistent. Emotionally, I no longer had goals or a direction. Only the ticking of the clock indicated that time was moving forward. It took great effort to move from one day to the next. Around others, I usually felt hollow, trying to act as though I wasn't just faking it. The challenge, which I would identify much later, was to build a meaningful life by integrating the past with the present, as a future very slowly took form.

Each day that I coped and survived I figured I was doing well. I felt a great deal of self-blame and shame for not somehow preventing Melissa's death. This added to the already high level of grief, so I worried whether I would be able to tolerate the pain into my now-futureless life. I could not imagine how it could be alleviated. As I contemplated these questions, I drifted, totally preoccupied with my misery.

It wasn't long before I discovered that my mind, without any conscious effort, had focused itself on two fixed points of interest. The first one was thinking of death as an inviting prospect. The second was experiencing a tremendous drive to understand what had happened to Melissa.

18

I Want to Die

In Greek mythology, Persephone, a young maiden and daughter of Demeter, Goddess of Agriculture, is suddenly kidnapped by Hades, God of the Underworld. When Demeter discovers that her daughter is missing, she feels a despair so deep that she cares about nothing else. Consequently, she stops all plant life from growing on Earth. It is only when Persephone is found and a compromise is worked out with Hades that Demeter allows plants to grow again. They agree that Persephone will spend the spring and summer happily with her mother and return to Hades in the fall and winter.

I, too, believed that my life could not go on without my child. The fact that Melissa was gone enshrouded me in unrelenting pain. Everything else in my life came to a halt. I felt as though my life from then on would be based on a raw emotion that I would not be able to handle. I didn't want to wake up in the morning when consciousness would remind me one more time that the worst had happened. I forced myself to get out of bed. Sometimes I had vivid dreams in which Melissa was alive. As I was having them I couldn't believe my miraculous luck. I felt euphoric. When I woke up, it felt as though the devil had played a sadistic joke. Demoralized and hopeless, I began another day.

Needless to say, the death of my child led to desperate forms of thinking. Expecting that my life would be filled with an intolerable pain that I could not endure, only the thought of my own death brought me peace. I felt less alone knowing John had similar thoughts, but it was also terrifying to imagine trying to live without him. Fortunately, these seductive thoughts remained just that, and never escalated into actions, because very early on John and I made a choice to live. We knew we would never abandon Brandon. I didn't know how we would manage to rise out of the inky depths; I just knew we had to. Nevertheless, these were serious thoughts that gradually became softer, less frequent, and eventually were heard as occasional whispers.

Another kind of loss wrapped itself around me: The ability to be free of sadness and be able to bring about my own happiness. I had grown up in the aftermath of several family tragedies, so it felt as though I had been exposed to considerable sadness by the adults around me, and consequently carried it inside of me into adulthood.

When I was five years old, one of my dad's favorite sisters died. On a bitterly cold pre-dawn morning in January my aunt left the farmhouse where she lived, and walked through the snow to the train tracks that ran by the farm. She left her sleeping family: her husband, bedridden with a slipped disc, her sister-in-law who was helping out with the family, and three small children including an infant. My parents told me that my aunt had suffered neurological damage due to complications during a previous pregnancy that resulted in lack of oxygen to her brain. No one knew what was in her mind when she put on her coat and boots and headed for the tracks in the middle of the night. However, my parents speculated that she was intending to catch a ride but was killed by the train instead.

Because I was only a small child, they tried to protect me from this heartbreaking experience; yet, through the years I became aware of various ways this tragedy rippled throughout my aunt's large extended family and into my own. Whenever the story of my aunt's death was retold or when my mother brought out the black-and-white newspaper photo of the winter tragedy, it seemed as though I could feel the wind's freezing terror on that early January morning so many years before. I knew it changed everyone's lives forever. It was impossible for my father to know that many years later his grandson, Brandon, would also experience the loss of his sister.

Four years later, when I was nine, a second family tragedy occurred. My mother's youngest brother and his wife had two small children. My parents were very close to them. My dad and my uncle went fishing and hunting together. I loved to spend time at their house because it was bustling with activity. One summer day, as my aunt hung laundry up in the backyard, her four-year-old daughter, who was playing in the basement while she washed clothes, accidentally knocked a gas can off a shelf. The liquid snaked its way to the hot water heater where it burst into flames. My little cousin was powerless against the flames in spite of my aunt's attempts to save her. She died a day later and my aunt suffered significant burns, leaving thick scars on her arms. One of the saddest images I remember from my childhood was the tiny footprints outlined in soot that had been left by the heat on the cool cement floor. Once again my parents were jolted by a tragic, unexpected loss. Once again, pain and sorrow reverberated throughout the family, changing everything forever.

Now, I have a deeper understanding of how hard it must have been for my family to cope as they courageously carried their sorrow day in and day out. I recognize that as a child I experienced many good times. Nevertheless, I frequently felt the heaviness of grief and sadness in my family. When I grew up and left my parents' home I wanted to find ways to have more fun and lightheartedness in my own family life. As an adult I thought I had partially achieved that.

After Melissa died, I was convinced that I could never create happiness again, because I believed I would never be happy again. Yet, I had to do what I could so Brandon could enjoy hope and happiness in his life. The impossible task seemed to be tolerating my own sorrow and at the same time supporting him. Decades after leaving home, I was facing the exact dilemma that I had wanted my parents to solve: How to have a happy, carefree family life when someone you dearly love has died. I had much to learn. Once again our life support came to the rescue, reminding me that I was not alone as I struggled for answers.

We fell back into the arms and good will of our friends and family, our life supporters. When they initiated outings, we did our part by attending as often as possible. We began to notice that we felt better when we were with them and over the months their connection with us made us feel stronger. When John started to feel a sense of pleasure again, he felt guilty because Melissa could no longer feel anything. He noticed that he found satisfaction in things he would hardly have noticed had she not died. In spite of feelings, good or bad, we trusted our supporters to keep us on track. This contribution was so critical. It was the starting point for this book, and a subject I will consider in detail later.

19

Need to Know

The second intense internal issue of this period was an overwhelming drive to understand what had happened to Melissa. I felt a deep urgency to understand why she had died. I found it almost impossible to accept that disordered eating behaviors were the sole culprit. The doctors didn't seem to share my doubts. They hadn't scratched their heads and looked puzzled. They seemed satisfied with the explanation that low potassium had triggered, directly or indirectly, the cardiac arrest. Of course, once the extent of her brain damage was determined, there was no reason for them to pursue the initial cause. I was the only one saying, "This just doesn't make sense." And, "It matters." One might think there would be relief in realizing no one else was raising questions. But there wasn't. I decided that it was up to me to start looking for answers.

In retrospect I see that I was driven by the profound, overwhelming unreality that on one ordinary Friday morning my child, who I believed to be healthy, was delivered by ambulance to the ER, never spoke again, and died twelve days later. I was also driven by a hidden agenda that gradually revealed itself to me. I was looking for clues that might exonerate me.

With no forethought, I transformed myself into a sleuth. For a time I felt like Sherlock Holmes. I appointed John and Brandon to the role of Watson. Suspense and secrecy became my operatives. With imaginary bands of yellow plastic tape, I cordoned off the areas I wanted to investigate. Feverishly I looked for clues. I collected and poured over every medical record and scrap of information I could find regarding Melissa's physical and emotional state prior to her death. I collected all hospital records and reports, read the autopsy report, talked to her most recent dentist and therapist. I wandered through medical libraries and collected stacks of abstracts and articles. John and I met Eric for breakfast many weeks after Melissa died and asked him questions. I talked with her closest friends. I scheduled appointments with experts on eating disorders. "Googling" became a frequent pastime at home as I learned more and more about sudden cardiac arrest and the effect of low potassium levels. The most sickening topic to read about was anoxia and the death sentence it often brings, though not necessarily immediately.

I told almost no one the degree to which aspects of Melissa's death seemed mysterious or how doggedly I was taking action trying to make sense of it. The little I did share with our life supporters was usually acknowledged without asking a lot of questions. I was appreciative. If I had felt pressured to answer questions, I would have given minimal information and tried to emotionally protect myself. The issues resulting from Melissa's death, involving severe guilt and shame, and thoughts about wanting to die, were too complicated and painful for me to share with most of my family and friend supporters. Those problems we worked on for a long time in grief therapy.

In *Black Seconds*, a novel by Karin Fossum, Inspector Sejer, while investigating the murder of a little girl, says to a suspect whom he is questioning, "We humans can cope with a great many things . . . if we only know why. Ida's mother doesn't know why her daughter died. It's difficult, you understand, losing a little girl. And later having to bury her without knowing why."

Although I learned much during my sleuthing, I never found satisfaction for my deep skepticism that the only reason she died must have been due to an undiagnosed eating disorder. I would not accept that her death might have been, in one sense, easily preventable. That thought took my breath away one more time. Nevertheless, my fervent mission for the true cause(s) slowly diminished over time. All the actions I took helped because I kept eliminating factors to pursue. Sometimes I told myself that I already knew the cause and was stubbornly not accepting it. I struggled in my search and wrestled with my guilt. What I did learn was how desperately a bereaved parent wants to understand how their child died and that they will go to great lengths to find out.

20

Eating Disorder

I'm oblivious to the year, the day, or the reason I'm running an errand. It's any day. It's been a few years since Melissa died. Automatic pilot has taken over and I find myself waiting for a red light at a well-traveled intersection near our house. Besides cars, all kinds of transportation and people converge here; from buses to bikes, from parents with strollers to hot, sweaty runners on foot. Gradually distracted, my eyes begin to follow a young woman riding a bicycle. It takes a couple of seconds for my brain to register why. The reason is that she is extraordinarily thin. In fact, it is the form of her skeleton that leaves a visual impression, similar to one barely walking out of Auschwitz in 1945. Femur and tibia push the pedals down, not thighs and calves. I think, *Why is she exercising, using up the little fat or muscle left on her body!? Clearly she must be deeply entangled in an eating disorder.* How does one understand this extreme but not uncommon phenomenon? I take another look at her and want to weep; to weep for her, and for all the others who suffer from eating disorders.

Throughout this book and in this chapter in particular, I am aware of wanting to protect Melissa from being seen by others through a myopic lens and from potential judgment. Nevertheless I write about this personal and painful subject with love, respect, and a sense of responsibility to everyone who has also been caught in the web of an eating disorder.

In the aftermath of Melissa's death, I attempted to deepen my understanding of how unhealthy eating behaviors can become life threatening. I read an array of books and articles on the topic and attended multiple professional workshops. The following is a brief definition of two of the major eating disorders, common symptoms and behaviors, and particular challenges parents face.

The *Diagnostic and Statistical Manual of Mental Disorders*, Fourth Edition (DSM IV), identifies two predominant types of eating disorders, Bulimia Nervosa and Anorexia Nervosa. Bulimia is characterized by "recurrent episodes of binge eating" involving either purging or non-purging. Binging involves eating a large amount of food with a feeling that the consumption is out of control. Purging is often the next step in the cycle and is essentially a means of getting rid of the calories that have just been consumed.

Persons with bulimia may not appear physically unhealthy because their weight may remain normal and relatively stable. However, serious health problems may develop and some can be fatal. At the top of the list is the dangerous effect that purging has on electrolytes. Electrolytes are the substances needed to conduct the body's electricity including regulating the heartbeat. The body's proper functioning is determined by these levels falling within normal ranges. When someone purges, one of several potentially serious electrolyte changes is a drop in potassium. Depending on the level, a cardiac arrest may occur.

Anorexia is a disorder in which the individual fails "to maintain body weight, at, or above, a minimally normal weight for age and height." Individuals with this disorder commonly rely on eating restriction to limit their calorie intake. This disorder also affects the electrolyte system and can lead to significant electrolyte imbalances.

In 2002 the *Journal of Adolescent Health* reported the results of a survey of ninth through twelfth graders as to whether they had engaged in disordered eating behaviors to control weight. They indicated whether they had used behaviors such as restricted eating, taking diet pills, using laxatives, vomiting and binge-eating. The survey revealed that over half of the girls engaged in some form of disordered eating behavior. The *Monitor on Psychology* (April 2009) quoted statistics by the National Association of Eating Disorders saying that at any given time, more than 10 million Americans report symptoms of an eating disorder. These include anorexia nervosa or bulimia nervosa. It is clear that disordered eating behaviors and diagnosed eating disorders are widespread. They are also dangerous and sometimes lethal.

In spite of the misery and health dangers that eating disorders bring, they are usually vehemently clung to by those who have them. Ironically, it is as though the individual believes that her life depends on the disorder. Therefore, those with these disorders usually want everybody to stay out of this aspect of their life, especially their loving parents who look at them with concern and suspicion that something is wrong. If confided in, parents might try to intervene rather than go away. Secrecy and cover-ups become strategies to prevent others from interfering. Concaved bodies are wrapped in bulky clothes in order to appear larger. Appetites, starved too long, may explode into episodes of ravenous consumption followed by waves of self-loathing. Calories taken into the body feel like a demonic possession. They must be exorcized without anyone knowing. Hours of exercise or some form of purging may provide temporary relief. However, a sense of aloneness grows as the disorder(s) narcissistically takes up more and more space, like the tyrannical ruler that it is, leaving the sufferer in a shrinking world. These disorders are so powerful, so internally driven, that they can seem as though they are out of the individual's control. Openness and honesty with others are abandoned. Trust, which forms the precious root system of all relationships, gradually erodes until only disbelieving looks and sideways glances remain.

The trigger for Melissa's cardiac arrest and ultimate death was considered by the doctors who treated her to be an undiagnosed eating disorder, though she had never been assessed, diagnosed, or treated for one. If I were writing this book solely as a psychologist, I would not state absolutely that Melissa had an eating disorder. Without a prior assessment and diagnosis I would only be stating my opinion. I am, however, writing in the role of Melissa's mother, and will say that she had an eating disorder based on my own observations and experiences, as well as those of family members and close friends over several years.

I believed that all of the lab tests taken in the hospital were accurate. I read the autopsy report and asked a pathologist to review it. When I spoke to him about one abnormal cardiac diagnosis on the report he said he did not consider it to be significant. The reason I am unable to believe with certainty that Melissa died solely from an eating disorder is because, from what I've learned, most people who die from an eating disorder are not able to function as well as she did, and often have long treatment histories, including hospitalizations. In other words, in my non-expert view, the probability of having a first-time lethal event, given her prior history, should have been miniscule. At the same time, that doesn't mean extremely low probability events don't happen. Those of us close to Melissa knew from observation and conversations that her eating behaviors were often unhealthy. My purpose in stating the above is to briefly explain that a mystery is attached to my grief—a nagging notion that Melissa may have had another physical vulnerability that played a role in her low potassium level or cardiac arrest—one that is too late to discover.

I am not sure when Melissa's eating disorder began. I only became aware of it when she was in late adolescence. By that time she was at college and away from home much of the time. During her freshman year we noticed that Melissa's body was significantly thinner. She was a diver for her college's swim and diving team. John and I became worried, wondering if her weight loss was the result of stress related to starting college. People often lose noticeable weight when under stress or during a major life change. We were somewhat perplexed, because Melissa had always seemed quick to adapt to new demands and changes. Yet starting college had been especially hard for her. We also wondered if she might have inherited her father's genes for hyperthyroidism (specifically, Graves' Disease) which can speed up one's metabolism and lead to significant weight loss, as it had with John when he was only twenty-eight-years-old. This condition had crept up on him so gradually that he didn't notice its symptoms. He needed to be hospitalized for a week by the time he did.

A few weeks after a diving meet, we picked Melissa up from the college she attended and took her to an appointment we had made at a medical clinic in the Twin Cities. She had lab work done and met with a dietician. All of her lab results came back normal, including her thyroid function. As far as we knew Melissa was in good health and we could breathe easier. It wouldn't be until after Melissa's death that I discovered other notes in her medical chart.

21

A Parent's Dilemma

After Melissa's death, I reviewed her clinic records. For the most part I saw that she had seen doctors at least yearly and that they had weighed her routinely, making a recommendation at least during one visit to gain weight. They also seemed to be monitoring her overall health through observations and regular lab tests. However, when I saw the dietician's report from the appointment relating to the thyroid test, I saw a note written in the medical chart, "Monitor for an eating disorder."

Because of confidentiality laws, we were not informed. Now I ask myself, *Who exactly was supposed to monitor this? Melissa?* I have no way to know if she was even given this information. It's possible that no doctor looked back to see it. It is also possible that someone did; this appointment was approximately eighteen years ago, before electronic charting made communication among health care providers easier.

My experience highlights a common obstacle for many parents when critical problems arise with their adult children. Confidentiality is a legal right for young adults. The dietician who recommended that Melissa be "monitored" could not contact us. At that time, Melissa may not have had an eating disorder; or, she may have believed she didn't have a problem; or, she might have decided that telling her parents would be the last thing she would do.

Some years later, after I had become more aware that Melissa was showing signs of an eating disorder, she went in for a routine doctor's appointment after which labs were taken. I later called the clinic. I briefly expressed my concern to a nurse. Just as I expected, he explained that he could not tell me the results because of confidentiality rules. However, he did tell me that her lab results fell within normal ranges. I remember feeling so relieved and grateful.

During Melissa's young adult years there were other times when it was apparent that her weight fluctuated. Her face never appeared gaunt, and much of the time she looked healthy. However, during a shopping trip, reality slammed me in the face when Melissa began searching for skirts in the smallest sizes on the rack. I could not deny that she had a problem. I felt terrified. I desperately wanted to say something to her, yet felt mute believing that one should never comment on the size or weight of another person, especially one with a possible eating disorder. Today, I want to believe that I would have the courage to talk with her about my concern much earlier than I did in the past.

Just as a parent does not have ready access to information regarding their young adult child from a doctor or therapist, so, too, the professional does not have access to potentially invaluable information from the parent. Sometimes parental concern is perceived as intrusive rather than supportive, overly protective rather than valid. Of course, sometimes hovering "helicopter parents" do complicate problems rather than work with others to solve them. However, there are many situations when parents could be of much greater help to their children than they are usually allowed to be. They have a wealth of experience with their young adult's patterns of behavior, mood, physical symptoms, and social interactions. Behind the majority of young adults with a significant problem are parents struggling desperately to figure out what to do.

There are two things parents can do for themselves at the very least. One is to get educated about their child's problem and get professional help to cope with it. The second is to offer crucial information to any caregiver their child may be seeing, even though the parent will not be able to receive a response without authorization from their adult child.

From the time I became aware of Melissa's problem my thinking wavered as to whether she had a serious problem or whether I was overreacting. Sometimes I concluded that I did have a valid concern, but then talked myself out of saying anything to her about it. An example of this occurred during the summers when Melissa came home from college. She had always been involved in athletics, first in gymnastics and then in diving. During and after her college years she continued to work out and eventually started running. She ran in the Twin Cities

Marathon twice. We had a membership at a local fitness center that all of us used.

What we noticed was that in the summers Melissa attended aerobics classes frequently. I'd ask myself whether it was too much and wasn't sure how to answer that. We also had a stationary bike in our house. There were times when she pedaled for well over an hour. Once again, when I suggested cutting back Melissa was not deterred and remained on the bike. Each time my gut tightened: I was barely aware at the time that exercising excessively was a sign of disordered eating behaviors. At the same time I still didn't know what the healthy parameters were. At times, when my anxiety rose and I feared the worst, I would calm myself by thinking, *She is just staying fit. She has always been athletic and has started running. How is this behavior so different from what any good athlete does? I also reminded myself, Melissa's smart and informed. She'll figure it out on her own. Maybe she'll outgrow it and it will just go away.* But the problem kept nagging at me—no, I thought, *I'm denying it, or I'm too cowardly to face up to it because I'm not sure what to do about it. What is the best course to take? If I bring it up to her too strongly, she'll get defensive.* Consequently, I rarely brought the subject up and defeated myself before I began.

Sometimes I'd rally and decide to get proactive. I'd ask myself, where should I start? I could call her doctor, offer information, and not even ask any questions—which she can't answer anyway. But wouldn't I be breaking my child's trust? If she found out she'd be furious. How would I have felt at her age if my mother had called my doctor? Maybe I should get help for myself, or consult with an expert to get advice. How quickly could someone see me? What kind of expert—a physician, psychiatrist, therapist? As I turned in circles looking for direction I felt completely alone.

It is usually true that if a person is to be helped they must first accept that they have a problem and then seek and accept the help offered. As a psychologist I have worked with clients around this dynamic for decades. However, the challenge seemed much greater when I was trying to help my child. It was impossible to take an "objective" view of the problem, to be realistic about how much change to expect and how much time it would take. I wondered how to approach Melissa about a problem she might not believe she had or didn't want to talk about. The stakes of waiting for her to "get it" and then accept help were unacceptably high. The fear was that she wouldn't "get it." Maybe she would never accept help. I felt panicked, knowing I had to do something to help yet fearing that I had a snowball's chance in hell of having an impact on her thinking and actions. I felt an icy unbending reality that my precious child was being stalked by something that could not be trusted to go away, perhaps for the rest of her life.

I tried as hard as I could to wriggle free from the feeling of dread. I tried denying reality, turning it upside down and reframing it. When I stopped, turned, and faced the truth, I felt as though I were stuck in a small tunnel, claustrophobic, in full panic mode. I wanted to cry like a baby in my seemingly helpless state. And that was exactly what I needed to do. I needed to stop fighting the truth and surrender to the reality that MY daughter had an eating disorder even though I felt terrified.

About a year before Melissa died, when she was in graduate school, she often stopped at our house to use our computer. We noticed that she would eat unusually large quantities of food. I once asked her if her stomach hurt afterwards and she said no. I felt confused. After observing this and other behaviors over the course of several months, John and I often had heated discussions as to what to do, if anything. When John suggested some kind of "intervention," as he knew was used at times with someone with an alcohol problem, I reacted strongly and advised caution. At the time, I had not read or heard of anyone doing an intervention for problematic eating behaviors. I did not want anything said that might shame her, make the problem worse, or damage our relationship with her.

John eventually talked to her, and she temporarily stopped coming over to our house. When I talked with her she cried and said she felt misunderstood by us.

As I reflect back on those difficult conversations when John and I were trying to figure out what to say or do, I wonder whether an "intervention" might have been helpful. (For example, our family could have met with her to express our concern and offer specific forms of support.) Though the notion seems interesting to me now, there is no way to know if it would have been a good idea, a bad idea, or something in between. What I do know is that if John and I (and Melissa) knew then what we know now, there would have been nothing at all for us to lose in trying!

Back and forth the pendulum of worry swung. When the problem worsened, panic rose. It was clear that action must be taken. When the problem lessened, there was time to relax. Maybe it would take care of itself. As the pendulum sliced another arc through time, it taught a lesson: Take nothing for granted in this moment until it has passed.

In *Terry, My Daughter's Life-and-Death Struggle with Alcoholism,* George McGovern wrote with honesty and painful insight about the death of his forty-five-year-old daughter from alcohol addiction. Her life ended tragically when she was found frozen to death in a parking lot in Madison, Wisconsin in December of 1994. He stated, "As I have traced Terry's life and reflected on what I would do differently with the benefit of hindsight…I would make a greater effort to share in her life and development…I would, if I detected signs of alcoholism, inform myself thoroughly about this disease and do everything in my power to get her into a sound recovery program as quickly as possible.…Once the disease had fastened onto her, I would stay in close communication with her, expressing my love and concern for her at all times…call(ing) her every few days in a nonjudgmental manner, just to let her know I shared and understood her pain."

McGovern's words reflect a clarity that can come to a parent only after the death of a child. All previously nuanced or qualified reasons for having done or not having done something are irrelevant. After a child's death the only thing that matters is one question. What could I have done differently that had even the tiniest possibility of keeping my child alive? McGovern continued, "I regret more than I can describe the decision Eleanor and I made under professional counsel to distance ourselves from Terry in what proved to be the last six months of her life." Having said that, McGovern believed that, "She should have been confined to long-term care with no opportunity to leave until she was in recovery."

It would be erroneous to conclude that help was not offered to Terry McGovern over a span of decades. Many people in Terry's life attempted to assist her and sometimes succeeded. At times she accepted the help being offered and worked extraordinarily hard in therapy and treatment centers. At times she reclaimed sobriety, herself, and her life, which included two daughters and a husband. Then she would be blown off course again by an incomprehensible force that led to relapse, leaving behind all who loved her. Emotionally bruised, I can only imagine how they, too, faced the unwanted task of putting themselves back together.

McGovern's story reveals many of the struggles and dilemmas of parents when a child of any age has a very serious problem. As with Terry, often these problems become chronic after years of tearing up and down the roller coaster of constructive and destructive actions. Hope provides the energy to reach the summit, but ends in complete demoralization after a hair-raising ride to the bottom.

I strongly identified with McGovern's words of grief for Terry. Most regrets can't be predicted. Parents are too deeply involved in the chaos of trying to cope with their child's problem. But regrets slide off the tongue with ease after a child has died, keeping in mind that there is no way to know if specific actions could have averted catastrophe. McGovern said he wished he had not distanced himself from Terry during her last six months of life and had stayed in frequent contact, expressing his love unconditionally and continually. This expresses for me the pain of trying to support beloved children while watching them self-destruct off and on for years at a time.

McGovern was also plagued by his own kind of mystery regarding Terry's death—that she was not discovered in the parking lot before she died. This was a very unlikely occurrence. McGovern talked about this to a friend who said, "George, in this tragedy, as in so much of our lives, the luck factor is often decisive."

I've always thought of my family as a "smart enough" family, as Al Franken's character, Stuart Smalley, might have said. In retrospect, I doubt that any of us feel very smart when we think of Melissa. Years later, John and I tell ourselves that we approached this problem with way too much caution. I understand why we did. One outstanding reason, which flashes through the dark like a burning arrow, is that we did not know our daughter was going to die. We thought we had the luxury of time to observe, talk, and support her. Ideally, we hoped she would solve this problem on her own by getting the help she needed. Or, even better, maybe the problem would just go away and all of us could live happily ever after. Her luck, like Terry's, had often been good. Then on one particular December day, it flipped like the random toss of a coin, creating a draft that blew her life out forever.

22

Grief: A Rugged Landscape

Each individual's grief is unique because of differences in life experience and in the circumstances of the loss. This means that the kind of support needed and the time frame for grief cannot be standardized. Early on in my grief I learned two general principles that helped me a great deal. The first was that there was no "right" or "better" way to grieve, as long as that way was not destructive to me or others. The second was the importance of accepting that other loved ones would grieve differently from me. This was challenging at times when I wanted to impose something that was helpful for me onto someone else.

John and I expressed our grief differently from the beginning. I immediately sought out books in order to better understand the phenomenon I was experiencing. I read poetry and memoirs written by parents who had lost children. I read books describing grief and loss and how to cope with it. Whenever I read something new, the sense that I belonged to an invisible group that I had never met grew as well. It helped me feel more grounded.

John never picked up a book. He quietly listened to me whenever I wanted to share something I was reading; however, it became clear that he did not find help with his grief through written words. He tended to express his feelings when he was by himself or with me and our life supporters. He also was more comfortable crying with others, while I usually didn't even feel the urge to cry. It was as though my tears had mysteriously dried up. John said he experienced a kind of reassurance from others when he shared his feelings with them. He, too, was weighed down by guilt in not having prevented Melissa's death in some way, so just being with others, having his tears and feeling their acceptance, gave him strength, even if it was temporary.

I am one hundred percent Scandinavian. It is John's opinion that I take "satisfaction from a profound sense of self-control." He would go so far as to call me "stoic." When Melissa died I began to experience myself as vulnerable, labeling myself as "pathetic," in no small part because I knew others were feeling badly for me. I didn't want to be on the receiving end of that kind of attention. I felt weak and powerless, with a measure of pride-induced humiliation. My perceptions were skewed. I interpreted much of the open kindness and support offered to John and me as a confirmation that we were indeed seen as tragic figures in need of pity and rescue. It was, therefore, a great challenge for me to accept the support of others, even that offered by good and close friends.

To quote John's perspective of me at that time, "Her father's shy sense of Danish pride surfaced over and over and only through extraordinary effort was she able to deal with the public nature of her pain. Yet she needed help and comfort from others and began to realize that she needed to proceed despite her feelings and instincts to the contrary. She began to accept with pleasure the open offerings of many friends and family. In so doing, Judy realized beyond any doubt that the generosity and love of others was neither conditional nor motivated by any sense of pity that she could detect."

"Newly Bereaved"

A couple of weeks after Melissa's death John and I began attending a series of grief groups. There we met a parent who had previously attended another grief group. She said that she intended to return once she finished up with ours. This was the first time I had heard of The Compassionate Friends. In the following pages, I will explore more about this organization's approach to grief and how it mirrored my own experience.

The Compassionate Friends is an organization whose purpose is to support families who have lost a child, as well as to support those who are trying to provide friendship and comfort to someone who has suffered such a loss. They have 625 chapters nationwide. On the Compassionate Friends' website, founder Simon Stephens wrote, "The Compassionate Friends is about transforming the pain of grief into the elixir of hope. It takes people out of the isolation society imposes on the bereaved and lets them express their grief naturally. With the shedding of tears, healing comes. And the newly bereaved get to see people who have survived and are learning to live and love again."

Although I never attended their meetings, I learned that they identify four phases of grief as defined and discussed by Dennis Klass in *Continuing Bonds: New Understanding of Grief.* These "phases" seemed to describe accurately my experience.

I will briefly describe them for grievers or life supporters who might also find them useful.

The first phase of parental grief is called *Newly Bereaved.* It occurs when the grieving parents experience "the realization of the loss of the child, and a recognition that a part of the self has been cut off." This was a time when we were emotionally free-falling, terrified, just trying to cope. This was a time when we needed every gesture of support that was offered.

At the time of Melissa's death, John and I were both fifty-six-years-old. We never expected to have to deal with a new identity crisis. This upheaval was especially confusing when it came to our parenthood. We had been Melissa's mom and dad, but after her death, who were we? In everyday conversations, people would ask, "Do you have any children?" Good question. I would ask myself, *Do I have one or two?* The present tense always threw me off balance, because when the question was asked, there was an expectation that any offspring would be alive. Should I have said, "I had two and now I have one?" That answer always seemed to diminish Melissa. I realized I wanted to still be her mom, and I still was, except that she had died. I experimented with alternative responses such as, "I have two children; one is deceased." Sometimes I just didn't want to deal with any follow-up questions or responses. Other times I would try to save the questioner from the inevitable emotional gasp by sliding over the question or being very brief and changing the subject.

With practice and experimentation I became more comfortable when asked this question. Yet, even now, I still pause. Now it's about deciding how much I wish to reveal to a particular person in a specific situation. I remind myself that I owe no one any information. I have a choice. I am so proud of both my children, and I never want to short-change Melissa by pretending to others that she never existed.

In addition to the identity crisis, I had to come to grips with the fact that Melissa was gone. After she died, I kept expecting to see her. For twenty-five years, her life in all its richness wove in and out of mine.

I didn't know any other life except for the one with her in it. For several months I felt like a teenager yearning for her first love.

As Joan Didion wrote in *The Year of Magical Thinking* in reference to the first year following her husband's sudden death, "Nor can we know ahead of the fact (and here lies the heart of the difference between grief as we imagine it and grief as it is) the unending absence that follows, the void, the very opposite of meaning, the relentless succession of moments during which we will confront the experience of meaninglessness itself."

Return to Work

The Compassionate Friends call the second phase of the parental grief experience *Into Their Grief.* Could there be a less definitive phrase for someone outside of the experience? And yet, it fits when you are inside it. This is the experience of parents continuing to grieve as they begin to deal with daily life, including work.

John and I were fortunate because we had life support at work. Colleagues and bosses made decisions that helped us in the gradual transition back to our jobs and with ready backup. They also required minimal energy on our part. This was crucial because our stress levels were so high and preoccupation with our crisis took precedence over everything else.

Grief sets life by a different kind of clock whose timing can appear to have stopped or to be barely moving. The griever may be so overwhelmed by a shaken identity, and by feelings of devastation and sadness and a collapsed life structure, that it may be impossible for them to know at first how well they can perform at work. At first, work satisfaction may no longer matter or seem important. Joan Didion quoted a priest who, following Didion's mother's death, said, "We might, in that indeterminate period they call mourning, be in a submarine, silent on the ocean's bed, aware of the depth charges, now near and now far, buffeting us with recollections."

There are some who return to work very quickly after a death for financial reasons. Some may feel pressure to return because of the nature of their work; others because they want to appear strong in spite of their adversity. After all, in a competitive world, those who spend too much time in the pit stop are bound to lose the race!

There are other grievers who desire the structure and busy distractions, and perhaps the human contact of the work environment. Maybe, for some, staying as busy as possible and letting time pass are the most helpful things to do. Still others may take leaves, short or extended.

When someone in grief returns to work shortly after the death of their child it is a time of emotional vulnerability.

I have learned there is no one right way. However, it may be helpful to consider several questions as one proceeds. Such as, what if one returns and is not ready? Will the grieving process get delayed and resurface unexpectedly at some later time? Will there be ways of grieving while at work? Are there people with whom one works who will be supportive? Will one have the necessary focus to carry out major responsibilities depending on the nature of the work? These are complex and important issues.

Our supporters were critical in helping John transition back to his professional responsibilities. In terms of the University's calendar, Melissa died at the very end of fall semester. This meant John had some time before he had to test his readiness to return to a classroom of students when the spring semester started. The chairman of his department had wisely assigned a very competent graduate student, Melinda, to function as a kind of understudy for him. She was also a warm and supportive person, helping John feel as comfortable as possible under the circumstances. This behind-the-scenes support provided just the fortification he needed at a time when he had no idea whether he might start crying unpredictably or uncontrollably during class. He had complete confidence that Melinda could gracefully move to the front of the stage at any moment if he had to exit.

John had to face a particular vulnerability every time he taught his class, given that most of his female students were close in age to Melissa. Any one of them might suddenly morph into his deceased daughter. This was an interesting phenomenon, which I also experienced. Even several years after Melissa's death, I still found myself seeing her face in other young women. I must admit that I tried to do this sometimes. An angled profile, seen from behind the right shoulder, a fair-skinned, lightly freckled nose, a blond ponytail swaying back and forth while running down the parkway, slightly almond-shaped eyes; there were many features of Melissa I spotted in unsuspecting others that instantly thrust the past onto center stage. The reward of pretending the stranger was my daughter soon turned to pain, as sharp as a slap in the face.

In the end, John succeeded in conducting all of his classes. He experienced much less internal stress because he knew he had a safety net, a life support at work, ready to catch him as he tested familiar professional skills in a much-changed, very vulnerable self.

My work environment supported and encouraged me to take a

short leave. Because I was a therapist it was important and necessary that when I returned to work I was professionally competent to function in that role. Emotionally, I needed to be available to others in pain, not preoccupied with my own. When I returned, my colleagues were very supportive. I knew that if I needed to leave work unexpectedly they would understand and take care of my responsibilities. I was especially appreciative when they assumed that I would not work during anniversary days in December, even though that meant some of them would have less time off. One way I supported myself during workdays was by taking short breaks in the quiet hospital chapel or the medical library.

By the end of a typical day as I walked out the door headed for the parking ramp, I would start to feel radically different. The role I had assumed during the day with all its distractions and responsibilities began to dissolve. I discovered that by the time I was on the road my feelings had filled all the space around me. Surrendering to my grief, I cried out loud. John told me that he experienced the same phenomenon after he left his office for the day. Apparently both of us had compartmentalized our emotions in order to function adequately even though we weren't aware of doing so most of the time.

Grief Lasts Forever

My grief is simple.
It is forever.
I am a mother.
My child is dead.

Despite my ability to carry out most of my daily responsibilities, I continued to feel different and separate from others, as though I was straddling two worlds. I hoped that no one noticed. There was not one thing that anyone could have done to change that feeling. The only time the separateness was alleviated was when I was with someone else who had lost a child or I read about someone who had. This schism was a constant reminder of the profound and lasting impact of losing a child.

The third phase of The Compassionate Friends' model states that as time passes, equilibrium is experienced more frequently and bereaved parents are *Well Along in Their Grief*. It is such a down-to-earth phrase, and quite unsatisfying at first glance. It sounds like a cop-out, as amorphous as vapor. But the implication of the phrase is clear: You have been bereaved for years, you are a seasoned griever, and you can feel free to stay in this phase as long as you like. I began to feel "well along" in my grief.

I had experienced multiple and intense feelings of loss, learned about the crucial need for support, processed my loss in grief groups and grief therapy, and developed a life in which I lived with grief daily. I felt more balanced. At the same time, I also knew that for the rest of my life I would continue to have to work with grief. I knew the future could deliver other random events with the power to set me adrift at any time. There would be no way to know how I would respond. Most likely my grief would reemerge furiously. Members of the Compassionate Friends say that during this third phase, "Rather than identifying with the child's pain, the parent identifies with the energy and love that was in the living child." If I were asked what proportion of the time a parent is able to identify with the energy and the love versus the pain, I could not say.

Even now many of my memories continue to evoke sadness and pain. At times I judge myself by thinking that I haven't progressed as far as I "should have" by this point; that I "should" feel Melissa's energy and remember happy times more often. When I'm more in tune with my darker feelings, I become defensive, saying to no one in particular, "I'll feel any damn way I want. I've lost my daughter, after all. As long as I live I will never, ever see her again. Take that!" However, I am also able to have memories that are pleasant or humorous and to smile or laugh when having them.

Resolved As Much As It Will Be is the fourth and final phase of grief identified by The Compassionate Friends. I immediately liked the fact that it offered a paradoxical time frame. Since I don't find the word "resolved" to be accurate as applied to the loss of a child, I can accept it in combination with "as much as it will be." In other words, this phrase (and phase) acknowledges the lack of an end point, which is my objection to the concept that grief gets resolved. It takes several years for a parent to be able to feel that they have arrived at a somewhat transformed state in their grief. I also believe that there will continue to be wild fluctuations in grief intensity. Anniversary dates arrive every year. Other losses, including other deaths, may blow in additional storms of sadness. Life in all aspects keeps changing and so will one's grief. Hope comes from feeling steadier, even as grief walks alongside it.

Sibling Grief

Brandon was twenty-eight-years-old when Melissa died. Prior to her death his energy and focus was on the future. He was attending graduate school, considering career possibilities and looking forward to the rewards of years of hard work. Megan had landed a good job and together their lives seemed to be humming along. They had no children at the time but had bought a little white house with blue shutters in a neighborhood that was welcoming to young families. Everything in Brandon's life flowed optimistically forward with the expectation that Melissa would be a big part of it. Brandon and Melissa had a close relationship. They had a keen understanding and a strong desire to be supportive of each other. When she died, Brandon lost one of the most important people in his life and was left with a future filled with gaping holes.

During the decade following Melissa's death, Brandon faced pleasures and challenges common to many young men and women. One of his greatest pleasures was becoming a father to a son and, three years later, to a daughter. After a few years, he and Megan divorced. When he remarried, he became a step-dad to another boy and girl. As he cared for his children and worked on stabilizing his newly blended family, he continued to build his professional career. Whether his life was going smoothly or was in complete turmoil, Brandon, unlike many of his peers, carried the added heaviness and emptiness of grief for a sister.

In many ways Brandon's grief experience parallels John's and mine. At the same time, the void caused by Melissa's death presents itself in other ways. Because Melissa was of the same generation as Brandon, she would have related to similar concerns that accompanied their particular stage of life. They would have had each other to rely on during times when one of them or someone else in the family needed support. They could have blended their families and experienced the pleasure of even larger summer vacations and holiday gatherings. Sometimes I imagine the two of them relaxing with their partners and children and telling stories of the latest family escapade. I can almost hear the laughter as it ignites and feel the warmth as it spreads out to all of us who might have been listening. In the following, Brandon expresses in his own words what it has been like to live without Melissa for the past ten years as his own life evolved:

Ten years ago I watched my little sister slip away and die. I have never felt so helpless and full of rage as during those few days when her body lived, but we knew she had left us. I had always been thankful to have been born when I was—an age full of scientific progress and wonders. And yet, there she was—lying in a hospital bed, her body breathing right in front of me. It was easy to imagine she was just sleeping and would wake up at any moment if we just said the right thing. We tried the smell of fresh coffee grounds, the sounds of her favorite TV shows, talking for hours by her side. I couldn't sleep at night, my thoughts tortured by a deep instinct to rush to the hospital and protect her. In the end, nothing brought her back. Medical science developed over thousands of years with billions upon billions of dollars and it was all completely, utterly useless. I felt deeply betrayed. A family ready and willing to do anything to help her, a modern hospital's resources at our fingertips, and yet it felt like the whole universe of human capabilities was completely powerless to save my sister's life. That was the time of helplessness, of powerlessness, and of rage. This is what her death has always been for me. However, her life is an entirely different matter.

Today, my sister Missy is an amazing, witty, and beautiful person whose life is about hope, human connection, and so many other things it's impossible to sum up in a sentence. Although she is not physically present, she is a very important, if bittersweet, part of my life. Even a decade after she left us, I still think about her every single day. Sometimes it's just a flash of memory or a moment spent wondering what she would think about something that happened. Other days it's a dream that she never really died or has somehow come back and it was all just a big mistake. But as time goes on and more of my life unfolds without her, my thoughts are often about what I am missing or what she never got the chance to experience. I can imagine what she might be like now and the things we might have done in the past ten years. However, she liked to surprise people and do things others who know her well might not expect. So I will never really know what I have missed, although I can be sure it would make me sad to know how things could have been.

In my living room there is a picture of Missy smiling proudly on that sunny June day when she graduated from college. This is a living room she never saw, in a house she will never visit, full of four amazing kids she will never meet. And yet there is her smiling face, a bright yellow sunflower pinned to her graduation gown, looking out into our house and smiling upon her nieces and nephews. It's comforting to know she wouldn't think twice about the crazy clutter of toys and baskets of unfolded clothes scattered throughout the room on most days. Over the past ten years, she would have spent many hours in that living room, playing with her nieces and nephews, sharing her many wonderful gifts with them—her wry sense of humor, her *empathy and concern for others, and her belief in fairness and social justice. The kids know her as "Missy" and know that she was my sister. The fact of her death at such a young age clearly bothers them, at least enough that they always pause for a moment in thought anytime her death comes up in conversation. Their lives are influenced by her because she lives on in me and others who knew her. But they have lost a great source of joy in their lives. My wife Ashley never met my sister, but has sat and listened to many stories about her. I am profoundly sad that Missy and Ashley never knew each other. I know they would have enriched each other's lives in many ways.*

Ashley and I chose to live in our neighborhood because it is full of families and children and close to good schools and parks. Families with children live on both sides of us. If Missy were still alive, she would have spent many summer afternoons, crisp fall days, and warm spring mornings with us in the yard, walking up to the park, or sitting in the backyard. Perhaps she would have had her own children over. These scenes would feel comfortable and familiar by now. Instead, the summer afternoons pass by without her. The sounds of parents chatting and happy kids bustling about do fill the air, but there is someone missing. Our neighbors may have heard me mention Missy's name or seen her picture in our living room, but they probably don't know much about her. They have lost something, too, over the past ten years the lively presence of a wonderful woman dancing at the periphery of their lives.

III

Life Support

"Would you tell me, please, which way I ought to go from here?"

"That depends a good deal on where you want to get to," said the Cat.

"I don't much care where"—said Alice.

"Then it doesn't matter which way you go," said the Cat.

"—so long as I get SOMEWHERE," Alice added as an explanation.

"Oh, you're sure to do that," said the Cat, "if you only walk long enough."

—Lewis Carroll, *Alice's Adventures in Wonderland*

23

Portrait of Melissa: Bike Trip

One day I decided to take a risk by fully immersing myself in one of my favorite photographs of Melissa. I wanted to feel close to her by evoking memories of a happy time. The picture I selected was taken during a bike trip to Lanesboro, a small town in southeastern Minnesota. It was August 1994, and John, Melissa, and I went there to celebrate my birthday.

The photo took me back to a perfect summer's day, hot and sunny, with a bright blue sky—a perfect "Melissa day." The trees were still deep green and their large leafy branches merged with one another like the draped arms of old friends. In the background were two white-framed houses standing modestly among a variety of shrubs and bushes. They were part of a tiny community that had a front-row seat for a perpetual bicycle parade. That was because the Root River Trail draws riders of all ages from miles around. Its straight paved path cuts through the middle of town like a narrow gray belt. As I continued studying the photograph, I noticed that at the moment the picture was snapped no bicycles were moving along it. There were, however, four bikes resting upright in a rack on a green median. I could almost see heat waves radiating off their shiny black seats.

The riders of these bikes were not in the picture. Most likely they were inside the restaurant, which was behind the camera's lens.

Earlier Melissa, John, and I had eaten lunch there. It was a perfect oasis providing shade, perhaps a cold lemonade or glass of water, or lunch followed by a piece of pie. This humble stop was acclaimed as THE place for pie. A local woman baked so many tasty varieties that it would take many bike trips to sample them all. When a diner finished, a delicious heaviness would set in and the thought of getting back on a bike seemed challenging.

It was in the restaurant that day that Melissa spotted a man with two little children. He was attractive and very fit. Melissa took notice of both traits. She quietly leaned toward me, commenting on how attractive she found young fathers to be when they were engaged with their little children. I privately savored this delicious secret. Looking back I still cherish that moment. It was one of those daughter-to-mother confidences, which most mothers don't take for granted. I also learned something about my daughter that I hadn't known. I liked knowing that she valued a man who involved himself with his kids. I valued that also.

After lunch we left the restaurant and relaxed outside in the shade for a few minutes. That is when I noticed Melissa looking at the man again. He and his children had also left the restaurant, and they were preparing to resume biking. Near the man was a small turquoise bike trailer with red taillights. Squinting, I could just make out the heads of his two little kids through the cutout window in the back. As he bent over to tie his shoe, his white t-shirt glowed in the bright sunshine. Beneath the dark baseball cap his toned shoulders, arms, and legs showed up outstandingly clear in the photo. To quote my then eighteen-year-old daughter, he was "very ripped out," and I'm sure her heart was beating faster by then. I had heard her use this expression before, so I looked at him again and totally agreed.

As Melissa continued to focus on him, I turned to focus on her. I could not resist my impulse to catch her in that unaware, authentic moment. So I snapped a photo. She was only a few feet away. The sun shone with full force on her face and silky blond hair, which was tucked behind her ears. She was a little overexposed in more ways than one.

When Melissa saw me take aim at her with my camera, she automatically responded by pulling her upper body back. She literally looked off balance. She had thought she could escape my lens but knew she was too late. Her eyes shut tightly, as she broke up realizing that I had just caught her checking out this guy when she thought no one was watching. Her private inner thoughts, which were often secret, had been revealed. Her mouth opened widely as she laughed at the joke I played on her.

When Melissa looked at the photograph off and on through the years, she thought it was funny because I had also managed to include in the background the man tying his shoe and his children sitting in the little turquoise trailer. She always had a great sense of humor. I loved the fact that the photo was an inside joke between us.

As I put the photograph back on the table, I realized that by taking a chance I had enjoyed remembering the bike trip. I felt closer to Melissa. I decided that sometime soon I'd find another happy picture and indulge myself again. I also noticed that I still had a smile on my face.

24

Taking Risks

The fear that I would not be able to handle my grief in reaction to Melissa's photograph was irrational. Another, but more extreme, irrational fear is called acrophobia, the fear of falling. People who have this fear feel it whenever they are on or near a high place. It doesn't matter that they are completely safe. They hate high-rise balconies, lookout towers, and even cliffs with guard rails. I'm one of these people. When I get close enough to look over the edge of a sheer drop-off, my body immediately becomes charged and tries to protect itself. Every cell believes it is under mortal attack. My brain automatically imagines my body helplessly falling as useless screams gush from my lungs.

One of my worst experiences happened some years ago when we were on a family trip to the Grand Canyon. As I started hiking down one of the paths into the canyon, I thought I was doing pretty well. However, after about forty-five minutes I came to a section of the path that curved around an outcrop of rock, and I couldn't see the other side. It felt as if, were I to keep hiking, some invisible force would thrust me into the gaping canyon and I would fall to my death. It was a terrifying sensation even though irrational. The writing was on the wall, so to speak; there was no way I could continue. On wobbly legs, I turned myself around and headed back up the path, scraping my body like a piece of sandpaper along the rocky wall.

I would have loved to be able to hike down to the bottom and explore the canyon while watching its pink, gold, and shades of ochre change with each hour of sunlight. Friends have told me that camping along the Colorado River at the bottom is spectacular. I bet looking up at the stars from a sleeping bag is too. I could probably go to therapy and rid myself of this phobia. Instead, I've chosen to miss out on certain "highs." In other words, I manage this irrational fear by avoiding situations that trigger it.

The way I experience my fear of heights reminds me of how I feel when I look deeply into photographs of Melissa. Except for a college graduation picture, it took me three years after her death to want to hang photos of her. Snapshots are tunnels into the past with slippery sides. I don't have the same intense physical reaction as with my fear of high places. It's not a phobia. However, there is an irrational sense that if I look at her too closely, which I actually want to do, I will lose my footing and, in a sense, fall into the picture, into the rawness of grief. I used to desire this. Now I sense danger and feel less defended. How do I usually handle this dilemma? I avoid looking at photographs. Recently I've started to wonder, "What am I really afraid of?"

As I began to dig deeper into these feelings, I thought of the trip to the Grand Canyon. I imagined I was standing on the narrow path again looking out across it and down into it. I thought about Melissa and losing her. My fear began to creep in. But this time I didn't surrender to it. My knees didn't start to shake. This time I felt my blood rushing with anger. I breathed in deeply, filling my lungs. I felt warm and strong and stood up straight. Into the immense cavernous space, I bellowed with outrage, "I want her back!" I shocked myself by giving voice to the thought that I tried so hard to suppress. The walls echoed my words. I got quiet after my outburst. For so long I had told myself that I shouldn't be thinking like that, especially nine years after Melissa's death; nor should I have felt such depth of anger, which must have indicated I was not accepting her death. Perhaps I had not progressed in my grief as much as I had thought.

I imagined bending over and picking up the heaviest rocks that I could lift. I dashed them over and over against the side of the canyon wall in front of me. Sweating and grunting with effort, the sounds of destruction, smashing, grating, gouging, and cracking brought me immense satisfaction. I felt physically potent in spite of an emotional powerlessness. Eventually I stopped, exhausted. As I sat down on the path, I noticed that the sun, that hot star upon which we depend, was transforming the walls of the canyon to a fiery red. I felt miniscule. And, yet, oddly enough, I felt as though I had grown. There was something about standing up to impossible odds, giving a voice to my deepest desire even when I knew I would fail. I had taken a chance, lost and survived. I felt stronger.

25

Grief Group

L ife support began in the intensive care unit at the hospital as our
friends and family repeatedly stood by us in our terror and despair.
As I've said, this profound experience was the catalyst for writing this
book. Whether given spontaneously or with predictable regularity, their
collective constancy held us up when we were weak and completely
vulnerable. Even after those early days, our original life support
continued, and we sought out three additional sources of support. These
included a grief group, grief therapy for John and me, and spending
time in the natural world. It was these supports that brought us back
to life.

Our friend, Joel, raised the possibility of using a grief group for
support. He was helped by the one he attended after his wife died. My
search for a group ended at The Center for Grief, Loss, and Transition
in St. Paul. Although I lived in the same general neighborhood, I had
never noticed it before. I had never needed it before. It was amazing to
notice what my ears and eyes were able to perceive around me now that
death and loss preoccupied me. I felt as if I'd tuned the radio to a specific
station without hearing static for the first time.

We signed onto a series of groups scheduled to start in January
2002. According to the conventional wisdom about the optimal time
between a loss and starting a grief group, this was starting very early. We
didn't care. We were desperate. We grabbed for anything that seemed as

though it might anchor us. We felt like balloons that had slipped out of a child's hand, drifting higher and higher in the sky, directionless and powerless over the wind. With such a high level of raw grief and intense longing we really wanted the pain to end—and we didn't know how to handle it on our own.

I also needed help confronting a nasty mind game that I was playing with myself. If someone asked me how long it had been since Melissa died I could have instantly told them the exact number of days. If I could say, for example, that she had been gone for fourteen days, I could also tell myself, "That's only two weeks—no time at all!" Quickly I imagined falling back in time, until I reached the day when she was last alive. For a moment I would allow a wave of unreality to lift me up in the belief that she continued to live and was so close that I could touch her. Inevitably, the crest broke, shoving me face-first into the brutal truth. Being with others who were also trying to accept the reality of their child's death helped me. Eventually, a time came when the mind game didn't work anymore and I felt worse when I tried.

Attending a grief group "too early" turned out to be the right decision. Entering the world of parents who had lost children of various ages, we found others just like us. At that time our pain did not lessen, but we discovered a place where we belonged. The other parents and group leaders joined with us and we with them.

Darkness, as always, came early to Minnesota that January. We parked near a funeral home that was a short walk to what we referred to as The Center. The front steps led to a simple two-story frame house. It was painted white with green trim. There was a sign on the front lawn, stuck in snow, declaring, "The Center for Grief, Loss, and Transition." Later, I wondered how many times this warm wooden structure had opened its door to people like us. It seemed as though its walls should groan from the emotional weight of so many sad stories. Yet, inside that simple house, the bereaved came looking for something. What was it? Why here?

We entered the porch and joined others moving in the same direction. Once inside a kind of psychological hush began to descend as we merged with our fellow sojourners. As we took off our coats, we also began to remove the outer layer of social pretense that we battled to maintain most of the time. It was exhausting to behave opposite to how we were really feeling. Leaving even a little of this burden by the front door with our coats for an hour and a half provided temporary relief.

In this mournful world, which seemed like the real world to me, I imagined us as refugees. As we began our march up the stairs to our group room, it felt as though we were barefoot, slowly moving as one down a dusty road. Some were in worse shape than others. Our survival was uncertain.

Real refugees are usually in search of safety, or at least less certain death, as well as food and water. I thought that what we had in common with them was hoping for hope. Hope was not present for some of us, although the desire to find it was probably why we had come to that house on that ordinary Tuesday evening. Hope was all we wanted. There was no point in turning back on the path. The village, our life, had been destroyed. Our life—which we built, loved, and thought could not be taken from us—lay in ashes.

Inside the house were those who worked and volunteered. They knew why we had come. They focused on us. It shouldn't be otherwise. So instead of throwing giant bags of rice or boxes of dried milk out the back end of a truck, they offered hot drinks and cookies and gentle words of welcome. We placed our check in the fee basket and finished our climb to the second floor. We entered the room on the right, which was designated for any parent who was grieving a child. The children who had lost a sibling met down the hallway on the left.

In that room for parents I learned many fundamental truths about the loss of children. One of the most startling was that the terrifying wind could take the form of hellish flames, burning a path through a mother's memory forever. I met the young mother whose three-year-old daughter died in a fire in her home while being cared for by her grandmother. The mother also had a young son. I wondered, *How does she get up and go to work? Where does she find the strength to nurture another child when she feels like dying inside? How does she answer all the inevitable, unanswerable questions that her other young child asks?* I could barely think about the anguish of the grandmother. *How does she go on?* I told myself that I couldn't.

The mother shared some of the ways she learned to live with her sorrow. A part of my brain took notes, to be reviewed later when my own grief was not as preoccupying. I learned from her that in order to survive she had to cry at work sometimes and ignore those who didn't understand. It couldn't be otherwise. I also learned that she was one of the cemetery people. When she visited the grave of her little daughter, she frequently carried a stuffed animal or the makings of a birthday party to be celebrated unabashedly right there on the spot. I especially learned that this mother, along with others I met along the path, demonstrated tremendous courage every time she arose to start a new day. No day was ordinary or easy anymore.

I also met a young couple who had lost two children, one young son and a baby daughter, in a random car accident. I could only silently gasp. Two children gone at the same time—I had no words. The mother, who had been injured in the accident, attended the funeral on a gurney. I asked the young father how his grief had changed for him since the death of his children one year earlier. I thought, *certainly he will have some clear-cut advice about where I'm headed.* He answered this question several times during the course of our groups together. He replied that the pain was not gone; "It's just different." I wanted to scream, *what does that mean??!!* At best there seemed to be a suggestion that the pain might not be as acute a year later. I was to learn later that a year in the life of a bereaved parent is a very short period of time.

In our group, the ages of the children who died ranged from several months to forty-five years. Prior to my own experience with losing a child, I had a vague and extremely false impression that the older the child the less pain one would feel. In other words, if one's child were an adult then the grief might be less. What was I thinking? That it would hurt less if your child was twenty-five rather than twenty or ten? I wonder what it was like for my great-grandmother who lived to be one-hundred-and-seven-years-old and outlived all twelve of her children? Even though most of them were older when they died, she was still their mother. How much accumulated grief and pain did she experience as each child left her? By the time I opened the front door to The Center that was one grim lesson I had already learned. What we shared in this group was the experience of outliving at least one of our children and the feeling that the natural order had been interrupted.

As other parents told the story of their child's death, it was easy at times to think about how horrendous it was and how it was so much worse than mine. If I, or anyone else, verbalized this reaction, the group leaders immediately, yet gently, reminded us that the experience of our grief could not be compared to another's. Behind their words was the reminder that each of our stories was uniquely precious. This helped us know that we all belonged in the group and the support it offered; the message strengthened our bonds with one another.

During group sessions we talked about what kind of support from others had been helpful and what had not. One group member explained that after his loss many family and friends spent lots of time with him, which felt very supportive. However, over a relatively short period of time, the visits tapered off until there were very few, and soon he felt abandoned. We talked about how grief could result in depression, which if untreated, reduced the ability to cope with the intense pain. A father, whose young adult son had died, spoke about the comfort he gained by frequently visiting his child's grave. He said he also found comfort when he noticed others were doing the same. It reminded me of an article I read about the late Elizabeth Edwards going to the grave of her sixteen-year-old son, who died in an automobile accident, and reading to him as she had done many times when he was a boy.

As the group time came to an end I heard the chatter of young voices from the hallway as the sibling group broke up. They were children of all different ages. I was glad they had each other. Gradually we merged and walked down the stairs to get our coats. The night facing us was dark and cold. Once we left the front porch, said our good-byes, and walked to our cars, each of us would be on our own again. Yet one thing I knew was that I would return in one week, and all that happened inside that house was a source of life support for me.

We attended two sets of the grief group, which totaled about twenty weeks. During the first several weeks we experienced no relief. That is not to say attending the group was not helpful. The ongoing rhythm of time, place, and sense of belonging helped give us strength to move forward for another seven days. Gradually we felt a little relief while we were in the group, but it did not last very long. Eventually, the helpful effect seemed to accumulate. Some might question whether talking about a sad and terrible event would be the same as obsessing about it and feeling unnecessarily worse. That was not our experience. In fact, we experienced the opposite.

As we attended weekly grief groups, we began grief therapy. Both of these settings allowed us the opportunity to tell our story of loss as many times as needed. Sometimes we told the long version, sometimes the short version, and sometimes a specific part that needed a closer look. In general, grief therapy was especially helpful in addressing complicated and specific aspects of our grief. Many grievers do not attend grief groups or grief therapy sessions and manage well. Given our set of circumstances we felt that we needed both. Each was a crucial source of ongoing structure and support.

26

Friends: Unconditional Constancy

Sometimes as I look back on the early months of grief, I picture John and me sitting on a wooden raft, barely moving along a listless river. Like Alice, we don't know where we're going, where the water will take us. We have no destination. All vegetation and wildlife on the bank go unnoticed. As the river curves, the raft moves closer to the shore. We spot old friends. As they get on the raft, it wobbles a little. I would like to say that it feels good to have them with us, but we aren't able to feel good yet; we can only feel bad. What I can say is that we feel less alone, and we want them to stay. Later, they will step off onto the bank again, and someone else will come aboard to spend some time. As our life supporters come and go over the course of several months we begin to discover that it is they who are sustaining us. As we drift, they are breathing life into us. Eventually, like children waking up from a long nap, we begin to notice our surroundings and to care, at least a little bit, about where we are going.

Ellen and Martin

Ongoing predictability stands out as one of the key factors in the following examples of life support. Each is unique in how the individual or couple interwove their own resources around us and our grief. I start with Ellen and Martin because they clearly exemplify life support over a ten-year period. It is also within this context and timeframe that I am able to describe ways in which our bereavement changed.

We had been good friends for decades. Martin and John had worked together at the University of Minnesota for twenty-five years. Brandon and their son, Aaron, are the same age, and attended the same grade school, junior high, and high school. Our families shared happy memories of the holidays when the boys made movies with a rented video camera. Their 1985 video "Coke Busters" was a favorite, starring Aaron's dog and a refrigerator. One October they turned our basement into a haunted house and some of the dripping blood (dried red paint) still remains. Melissa, who was three years younger, joined the boys when they attended summer computer camp together. Our families also spent time in a cabin on Burntside Lake near Ely, Minnesota. It was there that I took one of my favorite photographs of Melissa. She was standing with a large walking stick, wearing my aqua sweatshirt with John's red and black wool plaid shirt over it that came almost to her knees. She was eight or nine. With blond hair, freckles, and a smile, she looked like a small woods' woman, happy and relaxed in the natural world.

In later years, as Ellen and I became busy with our careers and the kids became more involved in school, eventually graduating from high school and leaving for college, we saw each other less often. We would, however, catch up with each other intermittently at University and social events. Yet, when Melissa was hospitalized, Martin and Ellen were beside us immediately. Like vines, springing from adjacent plants, our lives wove together, trailed apart, and eventually entwined again.

On New Year's Day 2002, six days after Melissa's death, Martin and Ellen called to ask if they could stop by to see us. Without hesitation we said yes and soon they were at our house to console us, homemade chocolate chip cookies in hand. As we sat in our living room talking with them, Senator Paul Wellstone and his wife Sheila came to our door with the same intention.

Paul and John had known each other since 1967 when they attended graduate school at the University of North Carolina. In Chapel Hill, Paul introduced us to Sheila and the two of them had been very welcoming to us. Soon we became part of the same social circle made up primarily of political science graduate students. I remember meeting their first son, David, as an infant while at their home. There was a lot happening for Paul and John as they pursued degrees. Even though we were not living in what was considered the "deep south," the schools had not been integrated and the Ku Klux Klan was powerful and feared.

Many people were taking risky political stands based on what they believed was right. Paul was one of them. He felt intensely about issues related to justice and was willing to put himself on the line, sometimes ahead of everyone else; sometimes at a potential threat to himself.

After Paul and John finished their academic degrees, they began their careers, and for some years we did not see one another. Eventually Paul accepted a position at Carleton College in Northfield, Minnesota and John settled in at the University of Minnesota. In the meantime, Sheila and Paul had two more children, Marsha and Mark. Our family had begun as well. Then in 1990 Paul became a United States Senator from Minnesota. Even after winning the election, Paul called John to talk about political science and politics every few months and to catch up on each other's personal life. In spite of the hectic life that Paul and Sheila led, they were genuinely warm people who made the time to maintain and nurture their relationships.

Now they, along with Martin and Ellen, were in our home with one overriding purpose: to comfort and support us in the midst of overwhelming grief. Being empathic and practical, both sets of friends wished to nourish us literally and figuratively. Before leaving, Paul and Sheila invited us to dinner at their house. For several days, Martin kept mulling over what he and Ellen might do to support us in an ongoing way. He came up with an idea, and suggested that we eat dinner together at a different ethnic restaurant in St. Paul every Sunday evening for a year.

It was several days after the visit that we held the memorial service for Melissa at Unity Unitarian Church in St. Paul. Once again Paul and Sheila, brushing aside any concerns they might have had regarding their busy schedules, flew back to St. Paul from another funeral in Duluth that they had attended earlier in the day. It sent a powerful message to us that their top priority on that afternoon was to honor Melissa's life and to be with us in our grief. They followed up with their dinner invitation, which was a delicious home-cooked meal prepared by Sheila. It was not surprising to learn, when the story behind their tragic plane crash surfaced several months later, that they were on their way to the Iron Range in northern Minnesota to attend the funeral of the father of a state senator. It was another instance in which Paul and Sheila showed that they understood the importance of supporting others, specifically, in times of loss.

Martin and Ellen's invitation—to try a different ethnic restaurant in St. Paul every Sunday night—turned out to be brilliant. At first the beauty lay in the simple fact that these outings gave us a momentum that moved us from week to week. However, when we went out with Ellen and Martin, we experienced the personal caring from friends as well. Although our pain was barely tolerable, their actions, and those of others, functioned like a sturdy scaffold, making it possible for us to construct a bridge to another life, without Melissa. Later, we would do more and more of the work ourselves, discovering that this long-term project would span the length of our lives.

Our first Sunday night dinner found us sitting in a small Kurdish restaurant in downtown St. Paul. The idea piqued our interest since neither of us had ever eaten Kurdish food before. Our grief was still so overwhelming that the experience was almost otherworldly yet distractingly normal. The food was unusual for Minnesota, releasing aromas of Middle Eastern spices combined with lamb, onions, lemons, and tomatoes. Sitting in this foreign, yet pleasurable environment, we felt as though we were immersed in a rich marinade of unreality. We didn't feel as though we had lives like most other people anymore, yet, here we were having dinner with friends as if everything was normal. Although John and I experienced and expressed our grief very differently, we both seemed to benefit from the incongruous mixture of normalcy and otherworldliness. John said he found the normalcy to be reassuring, softening his anxiety and pain, while the otherworldliness seemed to bolster his denial, reinforcing his irrational hope that the world that lay ahead could possibly be one in which deceased daughters were resurrected, a hope he was in no hurry to give up.

The winter of 2002 was filled with the usual short days and long frozen nights. However, our Sunday evenings began to take on a warm predictability. As Sunday approached, John or I would ask the other, "Oh, what time are we meeting Ellen and Martin?" If the specifics of the plans had not been finalized, one of us would quickly call in order to nail down the time and place. Ninety per cent of the time Ellen had already called and taken care of the arrangements. She made sure the ball was never dropped. She did it with love and flexibility, and as time passed, we became more actively involved with the planning. Again and again, around 6:30 p.m. on Sunday evening, we would park outside another Saint Paul ethnic restaurant. Just as we stepped out of the car into the cold night, we would spot the two of them walking toward us, smiles on their faces, surrounded by little clouds of steam. One more time, we were met with greetings and hugs, and most curious of all to us, with expressions of eager warmth that told us they actually wanted to be with us. Sitting down with candlelight glowing on the table, we would face them. Their eyes revealed a loyalty and their presence a constancy we could trust. Outside, a Minnesota winter wind might be slicing the night without mercy, but inside, we were oblivious.

For a while we would focus on each other, speaking of our personal lives and talking about past memories or travels. Some of our mutual travels had been to very hot climates, such as Israel. It was hard to feel cold when remembering a desert temperature of 108 degrees or eating spicy dishes of India. Although I never found words to convey the pain of losing our child, which took over everything and filled up our entire world, searching for and eating at these new restaurants with others temporarily pried loose some of the preoccupation with our misery. It also allowed us to look with interest at our broader neighborhood, our city, and at other cultures that had produced such varied and wonderful foods.

Our discussions, which were at first fleeting, later more leisurely, were about the restaurants and the food, about the countries of origin of the proprietors, and about the national and international politics relating to each of the countries. We enjoyed Thai spring rolls followed by curries made with coconut milk that seeped its deliciously rich flavor into the white rice beneath. Indian meals became one of our favorites. Each one was preceded by baskets of warm naan to stave off our impatient hunger until the chicken tikka masala or tandoori and other delightfully spiced entrees arrived. Other evenings we feasted on Italian pasta and sausages or meatballs, slid Mideastern lamb shish kebabs onto our plates, enjoyed the savory aroma of cinnamon or coriander in Morrocan tagines containing raisins or apricots, and sipped exotic vodka drinks while waiting for Russian borscht or a generations-old stew.

Ellen and Martin always treated us as though we were "normal"— interesting, strong, and functional. Whenever Martin seemed to sense that our grief might be looming too destructively, he would grab hold of us as if we were balloons threatening to float off into the dark. Each time he held steady, redirecting us back to the table by saying something quirky, making us laugh, or perhaps commenting on the delicious spongy Ethiopian bread with berbere sauce or the fresh enchiladas roasted in corn husks. He seemed attuned to the fine line between the deep waters of grief and the potential drop into the abyss of complete hopelessness. Martin, therefore, took a "better-safe-than-sorry" tack. He kept us focused on the present and, even if we might have silently resisted, like a good father he was doing something that we needed.

When a loved one dies, one also experiences many "secondary losses." These are losses that result from the primary loss. A "secondary loss" that John felt keenly was the fear that he had lost the chance of letting others know what a treasure Melissa was. John wanted others to understand how much Melissa had to offer the world and that she was a person who would have made it a much better place to live. Consequently, he simply had to talk about her. He wanted to make sure that others knew what a talented, kind, and loving person she was, and hoped that they could thereby obtain a glimpse of how profound our suffering was. She had only lived twenty-five years; however, she had developed into a person who made us delighted to be her parents. She had strong humanistic values, cared about the greater good, loved her friends, was ecstatic to travel at any time, was disciplined academically, and knew how to have fun. So, when others, like Ellen and Martin, allowed John to obsess about Melissa and her life, to idealize and brag about her, to exaggerate without knowing it, and to cry or laugh about her escapades, it helped him adjust to some of these "secondary losses." He sensed that some people were uneasy when he did this, but as long as they hung in there and indulged his unquenchable need, they helped him. This was only one example of a "secondary loss" that John strongly felt. There is an endless list of these losses that I expect we will experience for the rest of our lives.

Even though I was pretty oblivious to dates and times, except in an automatic sense, the planet followed its usual course around the sun while the moon circled the Earth. Consequently, days continued to fill up weeks and calendars were turned from one month to the next. As the first year of loss kept nudging us forward, subtle changes began to occur. Sunday night conversations with Martin and Ellen wandered more frequently into current affairs and politics. They became more personally reciprocal. In other words, we wanted to hear about what their son, Aaron, was doing, how Ellen's aging mother in New Jersey was getting along, and what kind of birds were coming to their bird feeders. "Have you seen any Pileated Woodpeckers this week?" I'd ask. Recently, when they told me they had seen a large owl in a tree near their home and Scarlet Tanagers coming to their bird feeder, I felt awed just imagining such beautiful birds. And, I admit, a little envious. As the nature of our time together evolved from almost exclusive focus on our needs to one of more balanced sharing, the sense of normalcy deepened. They still listened to us fully and to our stories about Melissa. However, they also began to talk more about aspects of their own lives while we listened with interest. We had become less preoccupied with our pain.

As we approached the end of our first year of Sunday night dinners together, I continued to feel "pathetic." Ellen and Martin never said anything or behaved in any way that suggested they saw me that way. I had given myself this label. Yet it took me a long time to trust that it was not true. It was as though a positive part of my identity had been damaged, that who I had been had not caught up with my changed life. I would think, *You are the mother of a deceased child.* Internally I would gasp. How could that be? In addition, I felt like a failure as a parent. I told myself, *You even failed to fully launch your child.* Along with this I was shocked to discover that I had lived with the illusion that since Melissa had made it to young adulthood without a major childhood disease, car accident, and drug or alcohol addictions, she had escaped the major threats and would outlive me.

Ellen and Martin helped to lay my "pathetic sense of self" to rest. I thought that as we completed our first year of dinners together John and I should acknowledge our overflowing gratitude by taking them out for dinner, our treat. When we proposed this, they declined in unison. Their response made it clear that our invitation violated their understanding of what these Sunday evening meals were about. The offer did not reflect the true nature of our renewed relationship. Usually, when one is in need and someone "does you a favor," you acknowledge it and then perhaps "repay" the favor. Also, the favor is usually an action with a beginning and an end. It is finite. Martin and Ellen's offer had evolved into an open-ended, infinite one. Our offer to treat them, though well-intentioned, missed the mark.

I was acting as though the need for ongoing frequent contact must end even though I needed the opposite. I couldn't believe that scheduling us on their calendar for every Sunday evening was not an imposition. When they reacted as though they had been a little insulted I was grateful and reassured that they wanted to be with us regardless of our tragedy and that I was not seen as someone "pathetic."

Ellen and Martin showed us that we were friends, and they were not doing us any particular favors. Despite the obviously extraordinary actions they were routinely taking, they made it clear to us, not with words but by their demeanor, that what they were doing was not in any way heroic or special. Yet what seemed phenomenal to us was the unspoken message: There was no end or limit to our grief and pain, and there would be no end or limit to their presence and support. From the beginning, they reinforced the twin notions that they knew we were different because of our horrid experience, but we were still capable of being and acting as multi-dimensional human beings. They treated us as if we were whole even though we weren't, and very gradually over time we surprised ourselves and grew stronger.

As of the writing of this book we continue our Sunday ritual with them. We have never tried to treat them again!

Nancy

Not all of our life supporters came in groups of two. John and I each had a close friend who was available to us beginning the day Melissa was hospitalized. As with Ellen and Martin, they stayed close by and kept frequent and regular contact over a long period of time.

When I received John's call that Melissa was in the Emergency Room and I should come right away, the last person I remember seeing was Nancy. I heard her voice telling me to, "Go, now! Forget about work. We'll take care of it."

I met Nancy through our work together in a mental health program in a large Minneapolis hospital. We worked side-by-side and had conducted co-therapy together for several years. During this time we became close friends. From the beginning of our tragedy, Nancy demonstrated that she would do anything for me that I might need her to do, and she was always true to her word. From organizing the flow of visitors in the ICU waiting room to staying up all night there with us, she remained a frequent and constant force of support.

Several months before Melissa's death, Nancy and I had planned a trip to Arizona for the following March. As the departure date neared, I wasn't sure what to do. I didn't know if I could emotionally handle a trip that was so far from home and from John. However, I also didn't want to back out on my friend even though she put no pressure on me to go. She and I talked about my insecurities. Nancy was very clear that, if I decided to go and later felt I needed to return home, she would understand and support me. Because I knew I could trust her completely, I felt more confident about going on the trip. As a result, I was able to stay for the several days we had planned and felt pleasure and interest in the things we saw and did.

This trip was also an example of the ongoing work involved when one is in grief. Over and over, on the way to resuming an altered life, one stretches one's ability to cope and manage through risk-taking.

However, when one takes on a challenge and also has a safety net and life supporters, one is less likely to feel overwhelmed and unable to cope.

Nancy repeatedly showed her personal and creative style of life support in many ways. On Melissa's birthday, the first year after her death, Nancy sent a large bouquet of sunflowers because she knew they were one of Melissa's favorite flowers. The bright yellow petals with large brown centers standing upright in a blue opaque vase remain to this day a beautiful and meaningful act of caring. Other years she took John and me out for breakfast to a restaurant called Maria's. It was a special place because Melissa had raved about and we had never been able to go there with her. Another year, Nancy told me that while she was driving through the Minnesota countryside she saw a field of sunflowers. She said she stopped the car and spent some time thinking about Melissa. This private remembrance became a gift to me as well because she shared it with me.

Nancy has been the kind of friend who has the emotional capacity to pause at any time we are together, and acknowledge her own bafflement that Melissa died. That acknowledgement is also a gift to me. She can comfortably dip into the dark realm of sadness and suffering of all kinds. Sometimes she talks about aspects of her own life that have been difficult. This sends me the message that she believes that I'm strong enough to be helpful to her. In so doing, we support each other.

Eventually in our conversations, regardless of how dark they have become, we turn our attention to other topics, often the ironic and funny parts of our lives. Then we have dinner and go to a movie. Nancy has shown a deep resiliency in the face of my grief. She never left me alone with my pain. She has always been available to me.

Tom

John and I had known Tom since the summer of 1966, when his then-girlfriend and later-wife Cathy moved into an apartment as my roommate. She and I had grown up together in the same rural Minnesota community, and we had known each other most of our lives. After they and we were married in the summer of 1967, we kept in relatively close touch. For almost a decade, our two families moved far apart and then closer together depending on where Tom and John were pursuing their academic careers. Their lives merged once they both had accepted positions at the University of Minnesota. From then on they were able to pursue mutual interests. They often played tennis, although John says with a smile that they spent more time at the net chatting than actually playing the game. They also loved baseball and were avid Twins fans. Although they had very different personalities, they laughed easily, often blending Tom's Norsk humor with John's Irish blarney. Once they showed up to have coffee with Cathy and me wearing identical purple plaid flannel shirts. Later, after Cathy and Tom divorced, we all remained friends and Tom and John continued to pursue their shared interests.

Tom was at the hospital day after day. Usually a gregarious person, he was uncharacteristically quiet. As we busily consulted with physicians and neurologists, updated friends, relatives, and acquaintances, Tom continued to remain quietly present. He was always there. He was with me the morning I heard the worst possible news—that Melissa's MRI showed there was no hope for a meaningful recovery. John and Brandon had stepped off the ICU at that moment. When I was told the news, Tom was standing in the corridor. He put his arms around me, absorbing the shock waves of my despair. Now I knew that my daughter Melissa was lost to me. Tom didn't say a word, he just held onto me as my hope slipped away. There was nothing else he could have done for me. He knew it, as did I.

Tom offered a kind of constancy that was as creative as that offered by Martin, Ellen, and Nancy. After Melissa died, he called our home EVERY DAY for at least five months, and regularly for another three or four months. Each time Tom would call John to ask how things were going that day. If John wasn't home or wasn't able to answer the phone, Tom left the same message. "John, this is Tom, just checking in. Call back if you want, otherwise I'll call tomorrow." It was a mere sixteen words. When John was home and available, which was almost every day at first, the two of them talked, sometimes for five minutes but usually for a half an hour or more. In John's words, they talked ". . . about Melissa, about my and Judy's struggles, about our guilt and unbearable longing to hug and talk to Melissa. He listened but he also talked, always conveying empathy coupled with hope. Hope for us as individuals and hope that some good could come of this tragedy." What John wanted was impossible—hope that Melissa could still come back to us. In a matter-of-fact way, Tom would tell John that this could not happen. Because they had a close and open friendship, John was able to listen to Tom when he offered realism. He served as a kind of emotional bedrock for John. The unstated message was, "It was awful, it is awful, it will continue to be awful—but you will survive and eventually even thrive." He did not offer platitudes, such as "it'll get better" or "it'll take time but you'll get over it." Nor did he say, "You're both strong." But like Ellen, Martin, and Nancy he acted as if it were obvious that we did have strength and that our strength was returning slowly. It was in this sense that he offered both of us hope, and his message got through. John doubted that he would ever thrive again, but at least he began to believe that he might be able to plod onward, perhaps doing some good along the way; in part because Tom saw strength in him and offered John his own.

Although Tom called regularly for John, he also talked with me, and his continual presence helped both of us. I received almost as much comfort and secondary strength as John did from Tom's calls and his messages. Tom's calls came to represent for both of us the message, "I know that tragedy has happened to you, I know that you are suffering, I'm part of the strength you don't feel right now. You owe me nothing and I am accessible to you at this time, as much as you need."

Tom and John's conversations gradually focused on the interests that they had shared for so many years. All aspects of Twins baseball became vital. John also found it to be important when Tom talked about aspects of his personal life, his ups and downs, sometimes seeking advice and feedback on problems he was facing. John noticed that he began to look forward to these daily conversations and to count on them, feeling anxious at the thought of not getting a message or not talking for a while with Tom. However, he had nothing to fear because it never happened. In addition to the remarkable commitment of time, energy, and friendship that Tom had already shown, he suggested that they should have breakfast together every Friday morning for a year, which they did and then continued even longer.

As these life supporters remained with us in a constant, predictable way, many others helped maintain our forward momentum with more spontaneous invitations. They continued throughout the first year and well into the second. I could fill the rest of this book with examples. Instead, what I hope will be helpful is to identify key elements they had in common so that anyone who would like to be a life supporter can keep these in mind as they develop their own specific ideas.

Here are the ways our life supporters helped us:

- Whether it was going to Cirque de Soleil or going out for coffee at a neighborhood coffee shop we were always asked if we wanted to go rather than being pressured to do so. We would have quickly distanced ourselves from anyone who might have tried to direct our grief by telling us what to do.

- Our life-supporters initiated the activities and did not wait for us to call "if we needed anything." We had no motivation to plan an event and felt no enthusiasm in anticipation of attending one. We performed only necessary tasks and used remaining energy to try to cope with our sorrow. Eventually, we learned that we benefitted from going out with others, as long as we paced ourselves.

- Once we agreed to an activity, our supporters also provided the energy to make it happen, including such basics as getting information about an event and obtaining the tickets, or arranging with our calendar—free as it was—to come over and cook dinner. Two friends invited me and another friend, who was also under a lot of stress in her life, to spend two separate weekends at their cabins. During the entire time, they took care of us by cooking the meals, serving coffee and chocolate chip cookies whenever we wanted, taking us shopping in nearby towns, and doing all they could to give us comfort for a short while. Each knew a great deal about loss. One friend had experienced the death of her husband after living with cancer for ten years; the other had experienced the death of her seventeen-year-old son.

- In certain situations, such as our friends' son's wedding, we were invited; our friends didn't simply assume it would be too painful for us to go. They left it up to us to choose.

- In many cases people suggested ideas that they thought we might enjoy. For example, friends invited us to go bird watching with them, to spot Red-headed Woodpeckers in the "Big Woods" and Tundra Swans in wetlands. We seemed to always feel calmer in a natural setting.

- When our grief was raw and we were vulnerable, if one of us went out of town without the other, we were always supported by whomever we were with. About a month and a half after Melissa died, John went to northern Minnesota on an annual cross-country skiing weekend. He wrestled with whether to go or not. He decided that he would tell two of his friends who would be there that he might need their support. He went skiing and was able to manage his grief because he knew he had people to turn to if he couldn't. In the end, he was glad he went.

Life supporters, in general, showed great empathy for our pain, yet were not overwhelmed by our sadness. They maintained a focus beyond us, which ironically also helped us. They lent us their strength, treated us as if we were strong and functional even when they knew we weren't, and stayed close rather than avoiding us. With their presence, energy, and big hearts they silently communicated that if and when we needed more help from them, they were available. What was required of us was to take measured risks and stretch our abilities to cope. By doing so, with the help of all of our life supporters, we practiced and strengthened our ability to handle our grief. In the end, after a long period of time, we did begin to feel stronger within ourselves.

John and I felt extremely fortunate to have each other's support in our grief. It seemed unimaginable to experience the death of a child as a single parent. Nevertheless, we were in the same downward spiral, overwhelmed with the same feelings of horror, guilt, and fear. Sometimes the most we could give each other was not interfering with how the other was grieving. I remember one evening, listening to John crying in another room. I didn't go to him. I had nothing left to give him. There was nothing I could do for him and he knew that. We needed strength from outside our relationship. Our life supporters reduced the pressure on us to be the exclusive support for each other. They also gave some reprieve to our family members who were also grieving and in need of their own support. We grew closer as husband and wife; however, this positive force was not primarily due to our own actions, but from our life supporters.

All forms of predictable, ongoing, and spontaneous support functioned as an antidote to the shock and upheaval we had experienced. All provided a "steady-as-you-go" approach. A woman I worked with whose husband died was told by a friend that she would spend her first year of grief in her car, i.e., on the move. She said it was exactly what happened. We had a similar experience. Every person who called just to check-in, every invitation to have coffee or dinner, kept us moving. Every therapy session and grief group added a motivation to get up each day even though we didn't really care where we were going. As others offered their energy and we accepted it, they gave us a sense of normalcy and a rock-solid structure upon which to attach the pieces of our emerging selves. John observed that "they altered the very rhythms of their lives in order to help us past the first ghastly years as we swung between heart-shattering sorrow and robotic attempts to keep moving, physically and otherwise. They did so without question and without need of acknowledgement, and made their actions appear effortless. They seemed oblivious that they might be doing anything particularly special or heroic. They seemed only to think that they were being good friends in an ordinary way."

27

Grief Therapy

Our life support, made up of friends, family, and our weekly grief group, was doing everything it could to keep us safely on the raft. However, our overwhelming desire for Melissa to be alive again and our tremendous guilt caused us to look for professional help. No one had suggested that we were at fault or should be blamed in any way. Everyone seemed to take at face value that a tragedy had happened and that it was due to horrible luck, not parental neglect or misadventure. However, I especially could not believe this could be true if people knew the whole story. As a result of therapy and continued interactions with our supporters, over time, I began to believe that others were not thinking less of us. This provided much relief and allowed me to begin to move away from self-inflicted shame and reduce the guilt we both carried.

Just as a therapist doesn't function as a friend, so too, friends and family members cannot perform the role of a therapist. It was not long after Melissa's death that we began to realize that we needed a professional to take a close look at our grief and see if there might be some way, anyway, to ease our emotional pain, and to start unraveling the dilemmas in which we were bound. Any benefit beyond that would be frosting on a therapeutic cake. Although we could not know this at the time, we did find frosting and life did become sweeter. But that would take years.

I didn't know, until I discovered the fact while reading, that our grief was considered "complicated." I understood that losing a child under any circumstance was horrific. However, I didn't comprehend how the suddenness of loss played a predominant role. Therese Rando wrote, ". . . while the grief is not greater in sudden death, the capacity to cope is diminished. If you are such a griever, you probably are suffering extreme feelings of bewilderment, anxiety, self-reproach, and depression, and you may be unable to continue normal life." These were all feelings with which I was struggling. In retrospect, it became much clearer why we needed a therapist and used that form of constant support for a number of years.

As we decided to pursue therapy, we sat among the rubble of our lives. Time was irrelevant. All we felt was dread and terror because we did not know how to live without our daughter. We yearned for her to come back from the dead. Despite our pleading, she would not. No matter how much we cried for her, she remained completely unresponsive, lost to a kind of silence that made mourners rock back and forth and rip their clothes.

The richness of who Melissa had been was gone. All physical bonds were destroyed, except for the ashes in small cardboard boxes, patiently waiting to be scattered—and those entombed in the green marble urn on the bottom shelf of a small black table in our house. We hadn't abandoned them. But there seemed to be little connection between them and the Melissa who had once been alive.

We contemplated in horror the huge gaps she had left in our family structure and daily life. No longer would Melissa drive up and park in front of our house in her red car with the unpainted hood that we all called "Stubby." It got its name because it was so short it kept getting lost in parking lots. Melissa couldn't afford to get the hood painted, but with an impish smile on her face she said she liked the way it looked. Nor would she ever open the front door to our house again, drop her chunky brown billfold, keys attached, onto the bottom step, look at John and me and say, "Hey kids, what's up?" Every time she said that, I felt happy and young.

Our sense of culpability was the other most potent and unwelcome aspect of grief. Although we both felt it deeply, I experienced it more intensely than John. It was huge and dangerous. It seemed as though all other aspects of grief could be consumed by this one issue. Although I was vulnerable in many ways after losing Melissa, it was self-blame that crystallized my need for professional help. At the same time I had little faith that a therapist could help.

Perhaps because of the sustenance we were receiving from our other sources of life support at the same time, we were more willing to try therapy. However, I dreaded telling even a therapist my real reason for coming in for a session. But shame, falling on me like sheets of cold, black rain, drove me inside seeking any shelter and warmth I could find.

Therese Rando wrote that parents often blame themselves in some way for their child's death regardless of circumstance. She also said that parents may believe that they ". . . . have failed in the basic function of parenthood: taking care of the children . . . " Although Melissa was hardly a child when she died, in my eyes, that didn't make any difference. I believed I had failed to take care of her and had failed in my responsibility to help her reach full adulthood. I had failed so badly at parenting that my child was dead.

Learning that other parents blamed themselves was a comforting fact, in theory. However, it didn't relieve our pain. I believed that most other parents were innocent even if they didn't think so. We were guilty. There seemed to be no apparent way out of the vicious cycle for us. We both thought and said to each other, "I want to be dead." Having previously decided that this was not an option, we stewed in our suffering. We believed that we would never be able to lift our writhing culpability off this tortuous hook. "How could anyone possibly help us?" we asked ourselves.

In spite of our pessimism, the idea of meeting with a knowledgeable professional, referred to by a respected friend and psychologist, planted a minute seed of hope that perhaps we might find a bit of solace. No guarantees, we knew.

At the appointed time, the door to the therapist's office opened. "Welcome," she said, giving John and me a pleasant smile, as she invited us in. "Jane" entered our lives of anguish, grief, and shame. She was a moderately tall, slender woman who had practiced psychotherapy for years. I sensed that her attention was already focused on us and on the problems that we had brought to her.

Through the ensuing weeks, months, and years, she became a benevolent director, a crucial provider of support and constancy as we played out our life's tragedy in front of her. It wasn't easy for me to let her know how imperfect I felt and to ask for guidance, over and over again, given that I am both a therapist and a reserved person. But the one thing I knew was that I needed help. The longer we worked with her the more we appreciated how well she knew her craft.

Each week we stepped into the therapist's world, trusting her with our world— dragging it behind us as we crossed the threshold into her office. To the right of the door, a desk fit neatly in the corner. This was where business was conducted and notes were recorded. She filled out a receipt for payment of service as we began to accept the choice we'd made by returning for another session. Professional books stood at attention against the wall across from the desk, and the décor was a blend of the professional and personal with a touch of whimsy. A circle of six-inch women danced atop a low bookcase under the windows; a sparkling wand hung patiently alongside a book shelf next to the couch. The wand, of course, reminded us that wishful thinking or belief in magical powers would not return us to the lives we had before we trudged through Jane's door.

We had been working in therapy for a few months. I headed for my usual spot, momentarily drawn in, yet still externally focused. My anxiety rose a bit as usual. I set my cup of water, which I filled from the machine in the waiting area, on the coffee table. I noticed a lovely crystallized rock sitting on top of the table, bringing to mind the natural world. Two padded chairs with alert wooden arms angled themselves across from the couch, forming a triangle. At first, John and I changed where we sat, sometimes a chair and sometimes the couch. Eventually, I began to consistently sit across from Jane in one of the chairs and John sat across from her on the couch. Jane consistently sat in the same chair.

Jane was calm, friendly, and attentive, tolerating our chitchat before gently directing us back to our reason for being there. The soft lighting made us feel warm and safe. Why not keep talking about anything other than death, grief, and how it was impacting our lives?! However, it was back to work. Any events happening outside of this room, as seen through the squinting Venetian blinds, were completely ignored. Once again we were the points of a tight triangle, focused on each other and on the pertinent issues related to the loss of Melissa, as well as other things that escalated our distress. Jane repeatedly observed and monitored how we were managing, and skillfully intervened when she noticed us adrift.

Loss Is a Family Affair

We began meeting with Jane a few weeks after Melissa died. At that time Brandon and Megan joined us in the sessions. Losing Melissa was a family affair. We were like pebbles on a beach in rough surf, never still, plowing into one spot and then another; partially buried, partly drowning. Our family identity was thoroughly shaken. Our family roles were scrambled and we all felt sorrow and guilt regarding Melissa's death. As our relationships tumbled around each other in an unsettled state, Jane began by helping us examine our shared past and gradually guiding us in imagining a future family life again. As we sat facing each other, she gently posed questions to help us begin to grapple with daunting questions: What would our family life be like without Melissa? A keystone, a family jewel, was missing. We talked about what roles Melissa had played in our family. Who would play them now? How would that develop? What would we do with sorrow infusing every holiday and family gathering? I worried that Brandon and Megan might not want to spend time with John and me. They, along with Melissa, had all been in their twenties together, sharing a youthful camaraderie. It was fun being around them as they joked and laughed and turned even their tough times into humorous stories; but now one third of the trio was missing. Megan had two younger step-sisters. I assumed family time at her parents' home would become a lot more fun and livelier than ours.

John and I realized we faced the danger of many additional losses, secondary losses, as a consequence of losing Melissa. We would have to work hard to remain connected even as we struggled to stay afloat in the sadness and pain. Family therapy, another form of life support, provided us with professional guidance—including the regularity of a time and a place—needed so that we could stick together as a family through the loss process and the reconfiguration of roles.

We had taken our family structure for granted. Now we were forced to realize how unaware we were of how our family members had fit together. We had been too close to see it. Gradually, we began to understand that Melissa had often been a kind of sparkly glue, helping to keep our family bonded. She could be very funny, entertaining us and telling quirky stories. She also had problems we worried about at times; some she talked about and some she didn't. Melissa was a spirited truth teller—keeping the hesitant ones honest and the bossy ones humbled. She added abundantly to the rich mix of our family's identity and pride.

These were just a few of the roles that Melissa often played, and in her absence the wind howled terribly. I had never consciously thought about our family as having an identity, but I could feel it start to fall away like tulip petals at the end of May. How would each of us, members of this family, find comfort and support within its arms again? Grief was so wretched and the void so abysmal. I could imagine us moving away, rather than towards each other, desperate for relief.

Self-Blame

As Brandon, Megan, John, and I continued to work on the many ways Melissa's death affected our family, it was imperative that we address our mutual self-blame. As I said earlier, my guilt was acute. I thought that others, perhaps even members of the family, might hold me responsible for not saving Melissa. I told myself, *I am a psychologist. I, more than anyone in the family, should have effectively intervened.* However, John also blamed himself. He often said to me, "I was worried but didn't take action when I should have. What is wrong with me?" What added to the complexity of this issue was that during the last several months of Melissa's life, she seemed to us to be physically and emotionally healthy. We often replayed every encounter we could remember having with her, searching for clues as to how we must have missed the obvious. Soon we were back in the vicious cycle.

All four of us knew that Melissa had struggled with disordered eating habits over the last several years, in different ways at different times. When our family began to open up to one another, we discovered that everyone shared some sense of culpability. During one of the first therapy sessions, Brandon made a suggestion that became the catalyst for reducing my burden. He thoughtfully and clearly reviewed examples of times when a friend or family member had communicated to Melissa that they were willing to help her. (Some of these we learned about after her death.) He then suggested that since the four of us blamed ourselves for not doing enough, perhaps we could share in the guilt. Ideally, I wanted to be rid of every last bit of it. However, if there was one thing that brought a little relief relatively quickly in the first months of raw grief, it was Brandon's suggestion. I returned to the notion of "shared guilt" thousands of times and it never failed to soften the edges of self-recrimination. This perspective also allowed me to explore and tolerate looking at questions of responsibility rather than completely hiding from them.

I know that if any one of us had pointed a finger at another, it would have been poisonous, threatening the life of our family. Even now, John and I are still haunted by our self-identified "sins of omission." We still wish we had done things differently. Of course, we have no way of knowing if we could have made a difference. But now, when culpable and ruminatively shaming thoughts present themselves, we understand them better and struggle less with them. We know they will go nowhere but around in circles. It was a great relief to bring this problem up to our therapist whenever it reemerged. It helped to know we didn't have to carry it alone.

From the first grief counseling session, Jane gently introduced the reality that Melissa was an adult. Adult children are and want to be in charge of their own lives. In our culture this responsibility is normal and natural. Jane seemed to be able to take on the mindset of a young adult, reminding us how invincible twenty-somethings can feel. "Melissa wanted to do it her way," Jane suggested to us years ago. I never forgot that sentence. I interpreted it to mean that Melissa was making choices and decisions on her own. But as her mother, for a long, long time after her death, I didn't hold her responsible for the decisions she had made. And when I lost her she had become my baby again, my little girl, my daughter of no particular age.

It took a great deal of effort to try on the notion that she had been twenty-five-years-old, in charge of her life and at least somewhat responsible for what had happened. One part of me knew this and accepted it and felt a tiny amount of exoneration. Another part of me imagined how stunned and appalled Melissa would be if she knew what had happened to her; how she would have wanted to be alive to experience her own life and all of ours. Imagining the pain of loss she would have felt if she knew what the ultimate cause of her death (probably) was . . . Suffice it to say there were no words. So regardless of which way I was thinking, I was never angry toward her. The sorrow and loss far outweighed any other feelings, except for love.

John and I continued in therapy well after Brandon and Megan left. One of the first things we discussed in therapy was the strong need we felt to be with Brandon and Megan at times. Their presence felt comforting. It was hard for us to speak the truth because we weren't used to asking our children for help. We were the parents, had each other, and took care of our own feelings. But something drastic had happened and demanded that we change that unspoken rule and reach out for help when we needed. If we didn't, we feared that we would become more emotionally disconnected from them and perhaps Brandon and Megan would feel the same. That was the last thing we wanted from our living child and daughter-in-law.

Scattering Ashes

Among the many things we worked on during our years in therapy was the decision as to when and where to scatter the four boxes of Melissa's ashes that silently waited in the closet of her bedroom in our home. John was in no hurry to decide. After the first couple of years, I began to fluctuate between feeling impatient to develop a concrete plan for scattering them and respecting John's pace. There were times when I thought, *Why weren't we like other people? Why, immediately after she died, didn't we place them in a cemetery or scatter them in one place?* I have since learned that there are others like us who have taken time to scatter the ashes of a loved one. A friend of ours told us, and it really helped to hear this, that when his first wife died, her ashes were left in the back of a closet for a year until his new wife thought it was time to move them out to make more psychological room for her. By that time he felt ready to do so. He climbed a mountain that had been meaningful to him and his deceased wife, and together with a friend, released her ashes.

In November of 2007, six years after Melissa's death, John felt he was emotionally prepared. He also felt clear as to where and how he wanted to scatter the first container of ashes. The thought of seeing the ashes for the first time made my stomach tighten. To see my child in a different physical state was hard for me to grasp. I told myself, "I will do this with my family around me. I will try to find courage remembering all who have done this before me." I learned that it takes emotional energy to let go of a loved one's ashes and that there is no right or prescribed time frame.

John and I and Brandon and his family packed up and headed for a house deep in the woods along the North Shore of Lake Superior. We picked this particular spot to scatter the first box because in November of 2001, approximately six weeks before Melissa died, she, Brandon, John, and I had spent a happy family weekend together. It had been very special for just the four of us to be together, given their ages and busy schedules. We had even gone to a store in a town nearby and bought each of them a new winter jacket. Melissa selected a sky blue puffy ski-style jacket and a hat of the same color with an explosion of velour strips on top. As of this writing Brandon still wears his orange- and gray-lined windbreaker as soon as it starts getting chilly.

I loved our shopping trip. It was as though they were just kids again and needed us, their parents, to buy them new coats for winter. On Saturday afternoon, we hiked to the top of a small mountain. I photographed the three of them as they rested on a dilapidated log picnic table. I took more photos of Melissa wearing John's ski hat, which made her look like an elf. She smiled broadly as she draped her arm around her brother's shoulder in a pose any mother would love.

Six years later John, Brandon, his oldest child Kieran, and I hiked up the same path to the same special place. The picnic table was still there, having survived six more winters. It would probably last many more. As the four of us gathered at the top of the hill, finding a spot where we could feel a breeze, the three of us who were adults took turns scattering the ashes. I read the lyrics from an Ani DiFranco song called "Carry You Around." They were probably meant to express the love between two adults rather than a parent for her child, yet the words expressed many of the feelings I was having. It was also meaningful because Melissa had been passionate about Ani's music while in college and copied many of the lyrics she loved in her diary. John read something Melissa had written. Brandon stood with us, keeping an eye on Kieran who quietly watched from a nearby granite rock. I brought a bag of several different-colored rose petals, which we used for the last part of the simple ritual. We each gently gathered red, yellow, pink, and white rose petals into our hands and sprinkled them over the ground where the ashes lay. Enthusiastically, Kieran immersed himself in this part of the loving ritual.

Birthday Ritual

At home there were still three boxes of Melissa's ashes to scatter in another place at another time. However, we had made progress that weekend and used our next session with Jane to decide where we would take the next box. We decided to scatter the ashes over tall prairie grassland that I had come to love. We would go in June to mark her birthday. I would keep my fingers crossed that the day would dress up for the occasion—that the big sky would turn the bluest it could be, and that the sun would shimmer golden white, blinding me for the second I looked at it before driving my eyes down to peer within the grasses for treasures of plants and insects. By that time I hoped my sadness would have been scooped up by the wind, riding the air currents like a kite above the prairie; transcended by the natural world.

We would also celebrate Melissa's birthday on the exact day as we had done every year since her death. Brandon always joined us. He had also made a point of celebrating our birthdays, Mother's Day, and Father's Day—and we appreciated this gesture, even when we felt emotionally dulled and would not have marked the occasion if left on our own. We always celebrated his birthday. In retrospect, I saw with clarity that these days of coming together were important in that they were predictable and brought us a kind of naturally occurring constancy. They helped in reconstructing our family—even though we didn't realize it at the time—because they provided us with opportunities to practice relating and celebrating with one another without Melissa being physically present. Losing the support and love in being together for these important days would have meant more loss.

During our time in therapy we focused on grief and other things that increased stress in our lives, yet the therapy sessions were not without humor. I don't remember the first time I noticed, but I discovered Jane had a sense of humor and a hearty laugh. By then we had developed a comfortable relationship with her and started letting her see more of our personal and relationship foibles. Over time she helped us work through several important issues from which we learned a great deal. At the same time she used her humor skillfully so that at times her reaction during a session filled the room with energetic laughter. Soon the three of us would be laughing. Jane was very adept at dancing with us through a wide range of emotions.

The one purely joyful event that we shared with her during the time we saw her was the birth of our first grandchild. Kieran was born in March of 2003. No family or their life supporters could have been happier about a new baby. Three sets of our friends alone put on baby showers. They knew the joy we felt and wanted to rejoice with us. It had only been fifteen months since Melissa had died. Our family was still painfully constricted by death; however, at the same time a brand-new life was challenging us to expand our hearts to receive it, sweetening the offer with a chance to share in his life and future. There was no hesitation. We fell in love with our grandson and each of the three grandchildren who were to follow. We accepted Kieran's challenge and gradually discovered that we were able to experience both joy and grief in our lives.

As the children grew, we all became aware that they had missed out on knowing Melissa as their aunt. She, too, had missed knowing them as nieces and nephews. Brandon would never be able to share his children and step-children with his sister and they would never be able to play with Melissa or any children, potential cousins, she might have had. It was a harsh realization. On Melissa's birthday, when Kieran turned three, Brandon introduced him to his "Aunt Missy" by telling him about her. It was one way that Brandon began to fold her into his family even though she was no longer physically alive.

Throughout each year we continued to develop new or altered traditions, trying to stay close to one another and to emotionally keep Melissa present. Those efforts helped to strengthen our family in places where it had fractured and became vulnerable. I knew it would be a lifelong effort.

The Therapy of Grief

Beginning at a time when our lives changed so much that they seemed to disappear, Jane remained as solid and unchanging as granite. She watched us with a keen eye, like a mother making sure her child didn't run into the street. She assessed, supported, and intervened. She knew that parents in the upheaval of grief, as we were, could be unpredictable. From the first session, she consistently approached us in ways that we found helpful. She approached us with gentleness, demonstrated great patience, expressed honor towards Melissa, and showed deference toward our experience of loss. In addition, she seemed to have a deep faith that we would discover unexpected resources within ourselves upon which we would gradually draw; and she continued to keep a watchful eye on signs of depression and self-destructive behaviors and thoughts. Jane provided us with all of this and so much more. With a pillar-like strength, she solemnly accompanied us into our version of hell. We trusted that no matter what we brought to her, she would not be daunted. She helped us enormously, and her wisdom and support remained as constant as one could hope for in this life.

The therapy experience provided us with life support and constancy, a soothing balm after being shaken to our core and knowing we would have to live with profound loss to the end of our days. It also served as a bridge from "then" to "now," delivering us to more solid ground. And as time moved on, it was one of few designated opportunities in which we regularly drew our daughter back to us as we talked and felt and remembered all of who she was. It was another way that we defied that terrifying imaginary ship, which carried Melissa further and further into the distance, threatening to disappear over the horizon. It was a place where I declared out loud, "She will remain with us! We will see to it!"

As a typical therapy session wrapped up, Jane said, "We need to end now." Another hour had passed. We had done whatever work we were going to do that evening. Even though we might have wanted to stay longer, this was Jane's therapy office and we were her clients. By ending the session predictably on time she was also letting us know that we didn't need coddling as a result of our tragedy and that she believed in us. Following her matter-of-fact directions, we grabbed our coats and remaining cups of water. Another session was scheduled and confirmed. Then Jane opened the door. We stepped across the threshold feeling less burdened. "Take care," she said, smiling warmly.

28

The Natural World

Every year after Melissa died we continued to celebrate her June birthday. As part of it we developed the ritual of driving to southwestern Minnesota in order to spend a few days in and around Pipestone. We discovered, over time, that it was one way of transcending our grief, even though temporarily. It was one way we could support ourselves without the help of our life supporters.

Pipestone is a small town with many colorful buildings constructed in the late 1800s. The colors of the stones come from pink Sioux quartzite, which range from rose to rich brownish red. This is not pipestone, however. Pipestone is quarried on the outskirts of town at the Pipestone National Monument. From 1937 to the present, the Monument has been open to the public; however, only federally recognized Indian tribes can work the quarries. The stone, pinkish to deep red, is soft enough to carve. The purest pipestone is very difficult to quarry, since it lies beneath the incredibly heavy quartz, which must be removed first. Legends say that no weapon is ever to be carved from it. For over 2000 years, skilled hands have quarried this stone and transformed it into symbols of peace called peace pipes. Several miles away is a small 590-acre prairie called Hole-in-the-Mountain. It is owned and managed by The Nature Conservancy (TNC). American Indians from this area called the valley "Mountain Pass."

Hole-in-the-Mountain was particularly meaningful to me because of my volunteer work for the TNC. During the three months following Melissa's death, I took a leave from work. I knew I would need a reason to get out of bed in the morning and have a daily structure, and since environmental issues had long been an interest of mine, I decided to search for an organization that might need the help of a volunteer. I lucked out when I contacted The Nature Conservancy, which had offices in the Twin Cities. They had an immediate use for me on one of their projects.

The people who worked in the office were very welcoming. It was an intense, busy setting, yet I felt at peace performing a very minor yet supportive task. I pulled specific kinds of property information from files and provided it to the team that was developing sophisticated geographical maps. Being part of this important project made my simple tasks meaningful to me. At the time the structure and environment were invaluable.

There I met people who avidly loved the prairie and all other critical habitat. Respect for and intimate knowledge of flora and fauna, and what helps them thrive, ruled in this world. And I observed to that end that negotiation, cooperation, and incredible persistence could move some mountains, at least. In 2002, after returning to work, I continued volunteering at a reduced number of hours. One day I was invited with several others to go on a late summer "field trip" to a prairie near the Twin Cities.

As the leader walked through the grasses of the prairie, she kept looking down and eventually pointed to a cluster of deep blue flowers. It was exciting, like finding the eggs of a ground-nesting bird. The plant, she said, was called Closed Gentian or Bottle Gentian. I learned they were unique flowers because the petals remained closed, like elongated blimps, unless a burly bumble bee punched its way inside. My introduction to the prairie surprised and delighted me.

I noticed over time that a sense of the prairie and its native flowers and fauna began to intoxicate me. I wanted more. So did John. As children we had grown up on the opposite edges of the same town in southern Minnesota. Both of us lived near woods and loved to explore, climb trees, and, in general, were fascinated by nature. When we started to explore prairie land, we felt a childlike thrill again. Our discoveries never disappointed.

One year we decided to arrive in Pipestone earlier than ever before and for good reason. I was in search of a native prairie plant, Prairie Smoke, while at its peak. Photographer Jim Brandenburg introduced me to these unusual native flowers in his well-known photograph, which I had hanging in my home. I have been in love ever since. It was true the blossoms looked like smoke, yet to me, I always saw little pink women with long tresses blowing freely in the strong prairie wind.

As John and I approached the fence at the entrance to the Hole-in-the-Mountain, I already spotted yellow wildflowers. I began to wonder what other discoveries lay ahead. From a distance, the prairie disguised itself as an uncomplicated, tall grassy place. It gave me pleasure knowing this was not true. I have learned that it takes several years of supreme care in order to establish and nurture a prairie. Of course, there was a time when we could leave that job to natural forces because the land had not been altered. I looked ahead and noticed the grass moving harmoniously with the wind. It bowed and swayed in a rhythmic dance. All was as it was supposed to be. Slowly walking through it, I felt my spirit expand.

The grasses were shorter and lighter green because we were there so early in the season. The prairie's rolling mounds climbed ever higher, urging me to do the same. From the top of each one the scenic perspective shifted. Small white clouds, which looked as though they had been shot out of a cannon, were the only interruption in the spreading eternal sky. Focusing my eyes on the ground, scanning the grasses, I anticipated with pleasure the discovery of color. I soon spotted a plump-petaled, purple and pink Veiny Pea. I had found a treasure. I felt happy.

Soon, an intense spot of orange caught my eye far in the distance. My binoculars confirmed it was a flower. It was hard to reach. No matter, I had to get to it and was duly rewarded. The tangerine essence, with a yellow center and freckles, belonged to a Prairie Lily. My discovery was blissful, and made more so when the photograph I took of the lily was brilliantly sharp.

I did in fact find clusters of Prairie Smoke growing in the prairie, as well. However, it was on the way back to town that I spotted a large patch of the pink beauties on a gravelly hillside along the side of the road. I looked at them with admiration. Those were tough little ladies with their flowing pink hairdos! As soon as John stopped the car I scrambled up the steep hill with my camera. I got close to the ground, took aim, and clicked my camera over and over again. I could hardly get enough. Later I felt full as I looked back at the pictures and remembered this weekend, this prairie with its hidden pleasure.

A few years later, in June 2010, we took a portion of Melissa's ashes with us to this prairie. We climbed to the top of the highest hill and found a large rock embedded in the soil and adorned with several yellow flowers at its base. As the wind blew in gentle gusts, the ashes were lifted and spread just as we wanted them to be. Although I didn't intend it, one part of the contents spilled into a tiny pile on the ground when the plastic bag suddenly collapsed. At first I felt as though I had been careless with the precious contents. Then I remembered that the natural forces of wind and rain would take care to disperse and blend them, folding them into the prairie forever. They would need no help from me.

As I looked up I could see a herd of buffalo far in the distance across the road. They were being raised like cattle, on a farm and inside a fence. They belonged on the prairie where we were walking, grazing on the grasses and sedges while leaving the other prairie plants to flourish, including the native wildflowers that I had fallen in love with. I wished they could enjoy this land as they once had, a time when they had the numbers and power to outrun their predators with tails flying in a full-force stampede.

As the wind kept the prairie waving rhythmically, my grief was soothed. It was as though Mother Earth was drawing me gently to her bosom for solace and nurturance and hope. The experience and feelings continued through time in my memories so I could draw on them later. I felt lucky to have found this way of transcending the heaviness of loss for a time. It was so right to bring Melissa here.

IV

Equilibrium and Transformation

I was something that lay under the sun and felt it, like the pumpkins, and I did not want to be anything more. I was entirely happy. Perhaps we feel like that when we die and become a part of something entire, whether it is sun and air, or goodness and knowledge. At any rate that is happiness; to be dissolved into something complete and great. When it comes to one, it comes as naturally as sleep.

—Willa Cather, *My Antonia*

29

Portrait of Melissa: Skydiving

After hugs and words of farewell, Melissa walked alone onto the jumbo jet. These would be her first steps on a trip that would take her over nine thousand miles away from her friends and family. Not one to cry easily, she did cry on that day. She was scared. Yet again, she had made a choice to tumble into the unknown of a new adventure. For the most part, she would need to rely on her inner resources to succeed. Melissa had decided that she would spend spring semester of her junior year in college at the University of Queensland in very sunny Brisbane, Australia. For one who celebrated the sun, this was a perfect setting.

In spite of the fear, her tears had nothing to do with changing her mind. She had bigger fish to fry. John and I believed that she could meet this challenge and also knew it would be hard. Although we would miss her and worry about her while she was gone, we also admired her greatly for taking this risk and later for successfully accomplishing it. Privately I thought, "I don't think I could do this."

One day at the end of the school year, shortly before Melissa was to return home, she called and told us of her latest adventure. It was wise of her to tell us after the fact; otherwise, we would have tried to talk her out of what turned into a thrill of her life. She informed us that she had gone skydiving. My heart skipped. What a kid! I felt a powerful mix of pride and anxiety.

She brought home a video of the entire event as well as a complete set of still photographs. I can almost hear the loud hum of the plane as I look at the small group sitting inside, all wearing identical blue jumpsuits with black straps attached. Melissa smiled at the camera. She looked very happy. What a moment it must have been! The anticipation of this fall must have been incredible. How could it not be—leaping straight out to greet the sky, racing toward the earth on the descent and the thrill of waiting for the parachute to open?!

Several photographs showed Melissa grinning back through thick flying goggles as she was free falling. All I could do was shake my head and smile. *That's my girl!* I was sure there was no last-minute gripping of the planes' door or second guessing a decision to jump. She was ready to take this plunge and was as prepared as she could be. She was probably taking special delight just thinking about how Brandon and I might react later since we both had height phobias. And so, the fall had been a thrill a second. The landing was perfect as the wide-open parachute gulped up the rushing wind on its way down, slowing her speed, with Melissa enjoying the final gravitational bump right on target. Just as planned.

I am grateful for every moment of joy she experienced in her life.

In spite of Melissa's spirited practiced and planned falls, there was one kind, I fear, she needed to let happen; a kind she couldn't control. This had to do with the times when she was bombarded with disordered eating compulsions and obsessions. My heart breaks when I imagine how she must have suffered at times trying to keep secrets, feeling alone, worrying about the stigma and all the other associated burdens. I know that if she had just let herself fall, there would have been a safety net, a life support, which would have risen to catch her.

30

Equilibrium

Simple Questions

They ask, "How are you?"

I stammer, expecting to respond with an easy cliché from the past. It won't come. I am a world away from being "fine." It is unimaginable.

They ask with searching eyes, "What can we do?"

I scan my brain. I want to say, can you perform miracles? Can you raise my daughter from the dead or put her ashes back together again? Can you explain to my husband where his daughter is right now? Can you help him accept that there is absolutely nothing he can do to bring her back; that there is no god or devil to bargain with and no one responsible? Can you tell my son that his sister will never play with his children or be his funny, wise confidante again?

Some ask, "Do you feel angry?"

I have no anger except that I have no answers for the most important questions.

Equilibrium came to me quietly and unexpectedly. The fragmentation I felt within myself began to clear up. One day in a therapy session three years after Melissa's death, John and I began to talk about how we were both beginning to feel more like ourselves. What was this we were experiencing? Why? On the one hand, it was a good sensation. I felt a little lighter. It took me by surprise, though, because I thought my grief had reached a plateau and would remain static. Feeling a shift in the process seemed strange. But this movement was not completely welcome. I continued to yearn for Melissa, though the intense daily sorrow that kept me preoccupied with her death had let up somewhat. However, this meant that now she felt farther away. John and I hated that feeling more than anything.

It was also disorienting to feel more like the person I had been before she died. I had been forced to assume the identity of a bereaved mother. I couldn't give it up even if I wanted to, which I didn't, because that is who I had become. I had been dragged through hell to accept that reality. But who or what was I now? Was I a psychological Frankenstein, with a past me jaggedly stitched to new emotions, coming to life?

There was not much to do other than to surrender to this altered state. Since I had not expected that my sense of self could shift after only three years, it began to occur to me that perhaps more changes were to come. I was presented with a crucial dilemma. If I was going to feel less pain in my grief, but Melissa was going to feel farther away, did I have any choice other than to allow this to happen? I realized that I needed to revitalize my relationship with her so that I would feel closer, and at the same time accept her loss rather than try to push it away. As if still in the womb, she seemed to move inside me, waiting for a rebirth.

Early emotional pain had been a powerful motivator. When the grief was so intense that it felt as if nothing else mattered, it was easier to take certain actions in order to seek relief. But when the feelings decreased, some of the motivation began to dissipate. Then I was left with another miserable feeling. My child was still gone and would be for the rest of my life. What do I do about the chronic hole in my heart? Like a boat that had just become upright, I kept adjusting the mast, sailing as best as I could with the ups and downs of a rolling sea.

A couple of years after feeling more "like myself," I read *Continuing Bonds: New Understanding of Grief* (Klass, Silverman, and Nickman). It helped me make more sense of what I was experiencing. Dennis Klass writes, "We can define grief as the processes by which the bereaved move from the equilibria in their inner and social worlds before a death to new equilibria after a death. Equilibrium is difficult to measure, but easy to subjectively sense. The parents in our study say that typically it takes 3 to 4 years before the new equilibria seem steady enough to trust."

Prior to finding this book, both of us had vehemently resisted explanations regarding how we should experience our grief. I think the spunky side of Melissa would have appreciated knowing that. Certain terms and expressions were frequently used in reference to death. One, for example, was that our grief at losing our child could "be resolved." We intuitively knew that it would be impossible to resolve our loss. It wasn't like coming to a settlement between a business and union over a work contract. Melissa was embedded in our lives and she was lost to us forever. Neither could we accept the word "recovery" nor the word "healing," which are two common words used to describe a healthy grief process. We weren't ill! Our daughter, not a hangnail, had just been ripped from us! The language didn't reflect the immeasurability of the loss of a child. Instead, it seemed to diminish the experience.

Most of our close life supporters did not use these terms or rely on other clichés. However, we frequently read them in newspaper articles and magazines or heard them used on the radio or television. They are even used in articles specifically written about grief. It is important to know that for someone in deep grief, language used by others to talk about their grief can be a sensitive issue. If someone, whose intention is to be supportive, jumps in with a pat "comforting" phrase, they may actually be revealing their own discomfort in the face of loss. The bereaved will probably sense this and may distance themselves in the future.

Obviously, this grief language never fit with my personal experience at the beginning, middle, or even several years later. Nor did I need those concepts or beliefs in order to foster hope in order to go on with life. Rather, the primary tasks for me during the first several months and years were learning to cope with the incredible pain and, later, searching for the threads of meaning with which I might begin to weave a future. So when I read the word "equilibrium" to describe what might have happened to John and me at the end of year three, I liked it. It fit. It was honest. I did in fact feel steadier and more balanced again in spite of the unexpected change. When others would ask how I was doing, I didn't stammer as much. It was easier now to say, "I'm feeling more like myself."

31

Transforming the Relationship

The sun is a powerful and ancient symbol of life. It has been worshipped by many cultures for centuries. The sun, in fact, sustains life on Earth. If it were suddenly turned off, we would crystallize, imprisoned in our last moment of time. When Melissa died it felt as though our sun, our bright star, was rapidly going out. In our fear and desperation, though, we kept moving and discovered something valuable. We learned that when we became actively and creatively involved in expressing our feelings about Melissa as a person, we seemed to feel a stronger connection to her. Our previous relationship with our daughter who was alive was being transformed into something new and different. Over time we developed paths by which we could reach her.

The Fellowship

Within two weeks of Melissa's death, we began to explore ideas for a memorial project. Melissa still felt alive but at an ever greater distance. All I knew at the time was that I had to keep moving and I needed to do something that made me feel as though we were carrying Melissa with us into the future. This thought gave me a purpose.

As we were getting started, we experienced one of the early duties of bereft families. It involved wrapping up all legal and financial matters. It was painful to feel Melissa's well-worn leather billfold in my hand, knowing that she had held it in her own hand four weeks before. It was disorienting to see her looking back at me from her driver's license photograph, to recognize her familiar penmanship written on checks and read the most recent expenditures on cash card statements. All of these items made it seem as though she were still alive. I also felt like a voyeur looking at information that I did not have permission to see. Nevertheless, this was a duty we had to fulfill and so we did. As we proceeded, the existence of a modest savings account surprised us. It soon became clear that this would become the "seed money" for whatever memorial project we chose.

Brandon suggested that we set up a fellowship to support a graduate student in the area of helping children and families. This idea was a perfect fit because it reflected much of Melissa's last two years of study in counseling psychology and expressed one of her strongest personal values. My son, in his usual thoughtful manner, had again offered a wise and useful idea that helped our grief move forward.

Before starting graduate school in the fall of 1999, Melissa had been employed as a personal care attendant. One child she cared for was a two-year-old girl, Raven, who had multiple disabilities. Melissa became very close to this child and her mother as a result of spending many hours with them in their home. Not only did she learn about practical issues, such as how to change catheters and manage frequent hospitalizations; she also learned about the individual, parental, and societal impacts of disabilities. She gained a wealth of insight and knowledge and often shared what she was learning with others, including us. This experience was transformative for her. In the spring of 2001 Melissa received a Masters of Arts degree in counseling psychology. By then she had gained even more knowledge and experience in the areas of helping families and children.

John was asked to give the commencement address at her graduation. He accepted with delight. As Melissa walked toward the stage, I caught her eye and we exchanged big smiles. This was a joyful day. As she walked across the stage to receive her shiny new diploma, she also received a hug from her father who was grinning with love and pride. He knew he was a lucky dad indeed! Six months later Melissa was gone.

By February of 2002, "The Melissa Sullivan Endowed Fellowship for Children and Families" was established. With the "seed money" from Melissa's savings account plus all the donations given in her memory, a meaningful legacy for her was begun. It marked one of the most significant shifts in the nature of our future relationship with her. To refer back to the simple sun analogy, one of the sunbeams became the establishment of the fellowship and the involvement in activities to support it. This was one way in which John, Brandon, and I, as well as anyone else who wished to join us, could stay in contact with Melissa into the future.

Memorial Tulip Garden

Another path of transformation was John's development of the "Memorial Tulip Garden." John had always loved tulips. Almost everywhere we had lived he grew them. When we moved to our current house, he started by growing a small patch of them in the front yard. Gradually, when he had time, he expanded it. However, after Melissa died, John blended his grief for his daughter and his love of tulips into an explosion of energy and creativity that resulted in a memorial garden for Melissa.

As each fall approached, John dug up more land, adding hundreds of bulbs, sometimes staying out until after dark. In June and July he poured over tulip catalogues, intent on finding new varieties, often coming up with new garden designs. Eventually there were over a thousand tulips. Color and texture flowed across our entire front lawn, spilling down the slope and onto the boulevard. John also extended the beauty by growing early, middle, and late bloomers. One day we came home to find an artist with her easel set up on the sidewalk painting the garden. We, of course, had to have the painting when she finished, so we bought it from her. It now hangs in our dining room. Soon people from all around the neighborhood strolled by thanking him for sharing such beauty. He told them that it was a "memorial garden" for his daughter, Melissa, who also loved tulips.

In John's own words he tells how his infatuation with tulips began in childhood and was given full expression as a tribute to his own child decades later out of love and loss:

It was an ordinary but stunning spring day. Melissa was taking her leave after a short visit to return home to work on yet another term paper for her ever-demanding graduate school professors. As she was leaving, she spontaneously expressed once again her admiration for the modest-sized tulip patch in our front yard, selecting a handful to take to her apartment. Although she might have seemed more practical than aesthetic in her instincts, Melissa was always drawn to the beauty of flowers and more specifically to the front-yard tulips. This image of Melissa heading home to her apartment with a small bouquet of tulips inspired me to create what has become known in the neighborhood as the "tulip yard" and years later, for me to be referred to as "the tulip man."

Although I was born on a farm, I moved to the edge of town with my family in the late 1940s. Despite technically being "in town" we lived on the edge of it, our property blending almost seamlessly with the fields. My family continued to maintain large flower, vegetable, and fruit gardens. As a child, I traveled door-to-door selling pints of raspberries and strawberries from the garden. These roots—in gardening as farming and commerce, aesthetics being secondary—led to a lifelong habit of gardening without the sophisticated landscaping or botanical aspirations of many urban gardeners. I usually described myself as an urban farmer, not a gardener. Melissa's death altered that, and much more.

Tulips are not necessarily high-status flowers among gardening connoisseurs. They are generally seen as easy to grow, a bit too showy and eye-catching, and even too commonplace, showing up regularly in the yards of casual or, even worse, non-gardeners. Serious urban gardeners typically prefer plants that are more difficult to grow properly and whose various features and attractions are more subtle.

I, however, have always retained very powerful positive associations with tulips, having been mesmerized by the sweet and tangy fragrance and the sheer brilliance of the "ordinary" tulips I grew up with in the late 1940s and early 1950s. To me, they were nearly the perfect flower, despite their non-utilitarian place in our garden. In those days and in our working-class neighborhood, neighbors were not nearly as interested in buying tulips as they were in fresh strawberries and raspberries. So I sold the fresh fruit, and simply enjoyed the tulips. I was delighted to notice all these years later that Melissa had a reaction to tulips that was similar to mine.

I think Melissa would be delighted to discover the beauty of the tulips and how they have spread, from the one garden she saw, with a few dozen bulbs, to several gardens with well over a thousand bulbs. I think she might also be a little amused, realizing that this was another example of seeing her father go "over the top" with one of his passions. Mostly, I hope she would be enthralled knowing that each and every flower was in honor and remembrance of her; metaphorically representing the shining brilliance of her feisty spirit, my boundless love for her and the all too brief bloom of her life.

Fundraiser and Donor Dinner

In order to grow the endowed fellowship, we decided to hold a fundraiser each May when the tulips were at their peak. We knew several people who were artisans and decided that an arts and crafts fair would be a fun spring event. In addition, John would have bouquets of tulips available for donation. We would hold it in our house and anticipated a warm gathering of friends and family.

Planning began in February when we designed the brochure and lined up artists who would participate in the arts and crafts event. Just two months after the holidays, and still winter, it was helpful to look forward to spring by working on this project. It gave me energy and focus. It also required that I reach out to others. As a result I could immediately feel that our life supporters were close by and willing to help in whatever capacity we needed them. Neither John nor I were naturals when it came to entertaining large numbers of people. We usually gravitated toward smaller groups and a sense of greater intimacy. However, hosting the fundraisers was the most ambitious and enjoyable transformative project I worked on.

At the end of March the brochures were sent out. On the cover was a tulip I had photographed from the memorial garden. It was maroon rimmed with gold, called a Gevota. This seemed especially appropriate since Melissa, Brandon, John, and I were all alums of the University of Minnesota and maroon and gold are the school's colors. All of the participating artisans and artists were listed inside. Soon rectangular display tables were reserved and decisions about what kind of food and drink to serve were made. By the first weekend in May, our arts and crafts fundraiser was ready for take-off.

On the day of the fundraiser, after many warm hugs and a few minutes of conversation, the shopping and donating began. For the next three hours, the main floor of our house became a bustling, mini bazaar. The artists stood shoulder-to-shoulder in front of the table where their work was displayed. They talked, answered questions, and laughed with potential customers.

A special treat was talking with several of Melissa's best friends who consistently attended the fundraisers. Their presence made her seem almost alive again. I felt as though they might lead me back to her if I followed them home. In my deep appreciation that they had attended, I usually didn't think about how coming to this event might have been helpful to them. John and I always seemed to be the recipients of support. Everyone seemed to focus on us. However, equally important was that others who had a history with Melissa, who also loved and cared about her, needed to express their feelings of loss. The fundraiser provided a place and a time to comfort and support each other. In this way the purpose of growing Melissa's legacy became partners with the important task of grief work.

John's youngest sister Maggie and her husband Mike had remained close to us ever since the beginning of the crisis. Maggie was the first person John called to join us in the hospital. He remembered saying, "Maggie, I need you!" She, who often felt like his baby sister, being six years younger, knew something was terribly wrong. She immediately came, and adeptly supported us in a way an older, almost maternal, sister might. This was exactly what he and I wanted and needed. Maggie and Mike sat with us in the hospital, around the long white table, holed up in a room, as we made the most horrific decisions of our lives. They stood with us around Melissa's bed saying what we thought at the time would be our final good-byes. They stayed as close as we needed during the next year and much longer.

When we began to organize the fundraisers, John and I knew we could count on Maggie's strength and enthusiasm to jump-start the energy needed for the event. Several years before, she had developed a process of preserving and reconstituting fresh flowers. She then artistically arranged them on "repurposed" trays, small wooden boxes, and table tops. Most of the tulip petals she used in her designs came from John's gardens that were at the end of their bloom cycle. Maggie had discovered a way of transforming the beauty of nature and giving a second life to the articles she used as her canvas. Her work was always sought out by those who attended the fundraisers. Consequently, each year she made a sizable contribution to the endowed fellowship. It was fun to watch her exuberance as she answered people's questions and explained her techniques. They would ask her, "Where do you get your flowers? How do you keep the colors? What do you put on top of the design to preserve it?" I remember more than one fundraiser during which she interacted with her "customers" for the entire length of the event and beyond.

Through her involvement she not only supported us with her positive energy in the planning stage, she also made the event livelier with her laughter and her warm, easy way with people. Maggie provided constancy every time, fortifying our own efforts. Our cause became her cause. Given a preoccupation with my own grief, I often neglected to remember that Melissa had been her niece. She, too, grieved. Her participation, and that of so many others, served as an example of how a loss can be a catalyst that motivates and channels transformative energy.

Our friends Lee and Joel, also, had been with us from the start and continued to contribute generously in a number of ways during the fundraisers. Lee, a creative clothes designer and skilled seamstress, brought her craft, her grace, and her style to each event we held. Each time, after Joel had helped her set up the table, she laid out her scarves of many colors. Next she hung dressy and flowing women's jackets and silky, stylish ponchos. I loved watching Lee as she modeled her creations throughout the event. She did this so gracefully one hardly noticed that she had changed into yet another garment. Some years Joel served as Lee's male model by wearing a shirt she had designed for men. Both of them gave generously. Lee's designs added greatly to the richness of the event. Every year they came and every time we felt that somehow they understood that their constancy was important and mattered to us. They were right. Every year they helped us feel more attached to others and to our life on this planet.

As of this writing we have been able to give out four endowed fellowships, each time reducing a student's financial burden while in graduate school. We know Melissa would be pleased. This was the time of year when she shone brightly in a transformative way through one of her legacies.

One word of caution regarding this grief work: There can be a form of "magical thinking" that infiltrates the process when least expected. An example of this happened to me immediately after one of the fundraisers. As I stood in the quiet living room, I realized, "'In spite of all the planning and flurry of activity, she's still not coming back." I, of course, knew that, but emotionally had been hoping otherwise. A great wave of sadness followed.

By September of each year, the tulip bulbs that had blossomed so deliciously in our front yard were once again beneath the earth hibernating, awaiting spring. Memories of our May fundraiser seemed distant. The brochures were filed away. The generous donations had been submitted and processed months before.

In October, a few weeks after the fall semester started, we were invited to the annual donor dinner. It was held to acknowledge those who had established scholarships and fellowships in the College of Education and Human Development, and to honor the annual recipients.

Emotionally, it is a difficult event for me because I am filled with thoughts of Melissa, and at the same time I am participating in an endeavor that I value, which only exists because Melissa died. As an undeniable reminder, the fellowship bears her name. It's on the program.

I looked across the table at the extremely grateful and deserving recipient who was our top priority that October evening. I knew my loss needed to take second place for a couple of hours. An internal battle ensued, which I covered up and hoped would subside shortly. As I talked with our new recipient, we started getting to know each other. I found out she had a boyfriend who was going to school in another city. This was personal information about which the motherly side of me cared. Our conversation helped because I gradually began to experience her as an individual, not as Melissa's substitute. Soon, the meal arrived, followed by a short, but meaningful program. It included several other recipients sharing how their financial gift was helping them; all of them were becoming more educated and developing skills that would allow them to give to others through the goals they were pursuing. By this time I felt more at peace. I was refocused on the purpose of Melissa's legacy. Also, I realized that, as donors, we were providing a kind of life support to our recipient, which then flowed out to the broader society, and returned to give our lives meaning.

By the end of this evening's gathering, even though I didn't personally know many of the other people in this large hall, I felt a part of a larger dynamic and reciprocal community. It strengthened my transformation process, even as I battled to quiet my conflicted grief feelings.

The Funky Room

In the late 1990s, following college graduation, Melissa moved to one of the western suburbs of the Twin Cities. Because she lived in an area that John and I visited infrequently, Melissa became familiar with a variety of stores and businesses that were new to us. One day she said to us, "Mom, Dad, there's a furniture store you would really love. It is called En Vogue." As Melissa had done so many times before, she led us to the threshold of a new world. This time it was the world of funky furniture.

Several weeks later, out of curiosity, John and I decided to check out this store. As we walked through the front door it was clear that much of the furniture was unlike anything we had seen before. We also fell in love with it. The chairs, love seats, and ottomans were upholstered in velvety bright reds, purples, and yellows. The colors alone made us feel happy, as though we were small children again. The whimsical styles seemed to belong to an ultra-modern fairytale. I felt like Alice in Wonderland when I spotted a lipstick-red chair in the shape of a shoe—a stiletto, no less. There were surprising love seats with backs that angled radically up one side only. To our delight, asymmetry was the primary design principle in this store. There were chairs and ottomans so big they seemed meant for giants.

As I tried out some of the furniture I felt like giggling. It was hard to imagine where any of these pieces could go in my house, although I wished it were otherwise. Even though it wasn't likely that we would ever buy anything, we knew we would return. It would have been impossible then to imagine that when we would return, Melissa would be gone and we would be decorating a "funky" room—and that the room was one way we were transforming our relationship with her.

In the winter of 2003, John and I began the second year of our grief. The need for the comfort and warmth of our life supporters remained strong. The profound effect of what they had collectively given us continued to be present even though we began to have less frequent contact with individual people. One day John announced that he had an idea. He said that he wanted to redecorate Brandon's old bedroom. It happened to be on the second floor of our house. He said he imagined a "coffeehouse" room, which would be warm, colorful, and welcoming; where our friends could come, have a cup of coffee or tea, and a chat.

At that time, our favorite coffeehouses had overstuffed couches and chairs, beaded antique lamps sitting on well-worn tables. Some had the ambiance of a converted brothel, with brightly colored walls or murals painted on them. No one staked out a table to work on a computer. No one conducted a small business via a headset. Those who came to these places, at that time, were usually meeting friends and drinking lattés with heart-shaped foam on top.

On the main floor of our house we had a living room and family room both painted white. Privately, I wondered whether we really needed another space in which to socialize. I wasn't feeling very sociable at that time, but I wanted to support John, and I thought it would feel good to work on a project around which he was so enthusiastic. As he talked about his new idea, he said he also wanted it to be an expression of Melissa's personality. My trepidation spiked when he told me the colors he had in mind. When John has a strong vision about something, he will "boldly go where no one has gone before."

He said he thought the current soothing slate-blue walls would look good if they were replaced by orange AND purple. My practical, all off-white decorating attitude snapped to attention. I knew I'd better get involved. I acknowledged that a coffeehouse décor in an actual coffeehouse looked great; but a room in my house?! Every conservative cell in my Scandinavian body screamed, *No!!* I panicked at the thought of bright colors on every wall, four of the walls painted different colors. Lime green and black were then brought into the planning discussions as well. How could I participate in this redecorating project that seemed to be driven by emotions and not design rules? How would we decide which walls would be orange and which purple? How could we prevent this creation from becoming a disaster? John seemed enthusiastic and confident. Was his idea fantastical or visionary? Whichever it was, it felt out of control to me.

After several more discussions, we selected a deep peach instead of bright orange and applied it to sixty percent of the walls. I could accept that. I felt more comfortable with the remaining walls painted a grape purple. By the time we painted the closet door a screeching lime green, I was completely onboard. By then both of us were having fun being outrageous. At the same time during this process, we did discover that there are guidelines as to which colors can be used in what proportions. That kind of information was helpful. I never would have predicted that I would love the result of John's redecorating idea, and that it would stand the test of time.

Once the room was painted it was time to buy furniture and artwork. The first thing we did was to return to En Vogue, the store Melissa had introduced us to years before. It didn't take long to buy two purple chairs and a fabulous round black rug with three purple ovals as big as dinosaur eggs and two squiggly shapes that looked like lime-green snakes. When we got them home they all fit the room perfectly. During the next several months we added art and a few more pieces of furniture. Soon a giant metal coffee cup with metal steam sat on a shelf of a tic-tac-toe-shaped black bookcase. A two-foot-high, whimsical purple animal with three long skinny straight legs and a crooked one, stood on the floor nearby. With delight we also hung a large mirror with a lime green frame, which created a spatial optical illusion. Soon the space we referred to as "the funky room" was complete.

The original intent of frequent socializing in this room never materialized. As in the past we usually visited with others in one of the conventional rooms on the main floor of our house. The "funky" room, instead, became a quiet, happy sanctuary. The two main windows in the room faced south, which meant that the deep peach walls lit up as soon as the sun rose. It was also the warmest room of the house. I was drawn to it like a magnet. Symbolically, it was a space of vibrancy, reminding us of Melissa, her humor and spontaneity. It was also a space in which we could help ourselves meet some of the needs that our life supporters had provided—a space to just be, to get lost in the colors and to smile as we looked around us. The "funky room" was a physical transformation that held within its walls transformative grief work.

John was also reminded that grief is complex and lasts forever. Even nine years after completion of the project, John said that as he looked around the room, he sometimes felt a deep sadness. He said that while working on the project, "I was always thinking of Melissa, trying to express her personality." He added, "I would love to show her this room. She'll never see it." He imagined her looking around the room and saying, "I think this room is really cool. I can't believe you and mom created it!" While he felt his grief very strongly, he also loved the room. The new creation gave him pleasure and helped him tolerate the sense of loss he felt.

These four paths—the Fellowship, the Memorial Tulip Garden, the Fundraiser and Donor Dinner, and the Funky Room—represent ways we transformed our relationship with Melissa in the past to a new and vital relationship we could have with her in the present and future. It took time for us to realize that this was the result of our efforts. With this awareness we could be more proactive in laying down new paths to reach her in the future.

I know I have not reached a transformed relationship with Melissa that will remain constant forever. I expect that I will always need to work on it. What I can say is that I feel as though I understand this process more clearly; and as the future unfolds, I can comfort myself knowing that my bond of love and unending pride can continue to be expressed, and that my ferocious belief in my daughter's uniqueness will keep her alive.

32

Living With Loss

After ten years of living without Melissa, one thing I know is that her absence is constantly with me. The opposite is also almost true. Her transformed self will be with me as long as I stay on the paths, or develop new ones. I do not think of her every minute as I once did. Nevertheless, so many things trigger memories of her that they are part of my daily life. Grief is now lightly scattered over everything. Yet, I am also not buried in sorrow as I once was. Because the sadness is painful, I still, at times, want to scream at it to leave me alone, as if it were something bad. But the fact is, grief is neither good nor bad. Grief is natural, a human cry in response to loss, a sign affirming our humanity.

33

Triggers

An unimaginable number of external objects and events trigger grief attacks. The triggers occur unexpectedly and frequently. The photograph of a smiling Melissa with a sisterly arm draped around her big brother's neck that hangs on my refrigerator, the bright blue necklace she got as a college graduation gift from friends, and the floppy-necked Barbie who lived in the attic for many years are instantaneous and piercing reminders of my loss. Since I have lived in the same house, neighborhood, and city where Melissa grew up, I also see the schools she went to and places she played and worked. Each one carries associations, memories, and feelings that have the potential to squeeze my heart. I've learned that this is how loss is.

Five or six years ago, I went grocery shopping for badly needed healthful food. It had been easy to gain twenty pounds after Melissa died. The misery I experienced at the end of most days seduced me into thinking that food would make me feel better; and, so it had in the moment, spoonful by spoonful. I was not alone. John was by my side.

On almost any evening it had been very difficult to come up with a good reason not to go out to eat. Or, if one of us was experiencing a little impulse control it quickly vanished when the other asked, "Have you cooked anything?" This was followed by a very short pause, blank faces, and then guilty smiles. "Where should we go?" "Let's sit outside somewhere; it's so nice."

Once settled at an outdoor table, a cool, dark beer and an icy green Appletini sitting before us, a sense of relaxation swaddled us. At first in our grief, even a sip of wine quickly lowered our ability to handle the depression. Later, we managed better, although I noticed that even five years later one of us would tear up when we spoke Melissa's name or shared a memory out loud. Anything that lowered our inhibitions left us more vulnerable. Soon foods that I had not ordered for years became standard requests. I couldn't believe I was hearing myself say, "Yes, I'll have a basket of fries with that burger." Why not? Yum!

Oh, those hundreds of early summer suppers sitting under an umbrella at one of our favorite places, across from each other, soaking in comfort by the waterfall and tropical plants, watching orange fish in the pond waving their diaphanous tails like beauty queens. These were our favorite days in this cold climate, when the sun refused to set and warm breezes lulled us like sleepy babies. I began to imagine we were on a holiday in Greece or Italy, Paris or Madrid. We sipped our drinks, dipped bread slowly in olive oil while savoring a fresh salad. At that moment, my focus was whether to order steak, steamed mussels in garlic broth, or a more exotic dish with a fusion of ethnic flavors. I was transported. I was cosmopolitan. I was not there. I felt good.

If I floated along in that pleasant experience, and did not drop my hand beneath the surface, I could almost feel as though my child was alive. And so, the illusory benign dining was followed by the ancient driving principles of the yin and the yang. With a little saltiness left on my tongue from a large plate of lightly battered, deep fried calamari, I had an overriding desire for sweetness, chocolate, ice cream. Fresh fruit was not what I desired.

Before we had been brought our bill for the meal, one of us posed the next question. "Which ice cream shop should we go to? Izzy's, or Grande Ole Creamery?" I thought to myself, our city was so blessed! Many evenings we stood in long lines selecting our favorite ice cream flavors. Often, by the time it was my turn to order, any resolve I might have had to order a sorbet or a single dip of ice cream in a cup had dissipated. Rather, I ordered a shake with "extra chocolate, please"; and, "yes, I'll have whipped cream as well." John, without hesitation, ordered the same.

So, here I am, back in the grocery store pushing my cart, satisfied that I have shopped wisely. I have a renewed commitment to better eating; there will be no u-turns to revisit the ice cream freezers or the aisle with small stacks of my favorite dark-chocolate-with-almonds candy bar.

Determined, I head for the checkout line. Suddenly a child's voice breaks my focus. "Mama," I hear from a few feet away. A little boy about five-years-old is trying to get his mother's attention. A younger brother sits in a little plastic pushcart, which is a perfect size for holding him. A child is calling for his mother. I feel a sudden thump on my sternum, like a knock on a door. If I pay attention for very long, a pressure I'm very familiar with will grow in my forehead between my eyes. Could that be the part of the brain that holds the headwaters of our tears? Spocklike, I have decided to analyze my tears rather than allow them. Rigidly I continue walking to the check-out counter. Memories have already entrapped me. Transfixed by their sights and sounds I've fallen back in time. I'm in my bedroom, getting ready to go out for dinner with the family. I hear a clear, "Mom?" as Melissa walks in. "Do you have a sweater I can borrow?"

For a long time after Melissa died, I could still hear her voice in the short hallway leading into our bedroom saying, "Mom?" I loved that sound. I loved being her mother. I'm envious of all the mothers who can still hear their children call for them.

34

Changing Traditions

As anyone who has lost someone they love knows, anniversary dates can trigger powerful feelings. Because Melissa died on the 26th of December, after twelve days in a coma and during the holiday season, that is the month that delivers the hardest punch.

As we approached the end of our first year of grief, the Christmas holidays loomed ahead. We had a myriad of feelings but none that had anything to do with celebrating. The next several weeks seemed impossible to navigate. So we decided not to try. We left the state, in more ways than one. We wanted to break all associations with the previous year and to divorce ourselves from any expectation to appear happy that Christmas was coming.

We knew, on some level, that we were not running away from our grief. We were functioning, going to work, getting therapeutic help and support from many sources and attending to friends and family. We did depend more on others to initiate activities, although we usually went when invited and thereby stayed quite active in spite of how devastated we felt. Also, at times we began to develop a tiny spark of hope that in the future we might learn how to manage and tolerate the emotional pain that we carried.

There seemed to be some movement in our grief—but there would definitely not be a Christmas celebration. We asked ourselves, where could we go in December that was sunny and warm—prerequisites for comfort—and where no one would care if we celebrated the holidays or not? Where might others be somewhat oblivious to the usual rituals? We chose Key West. It was perfect for our purposes.

We were helped immensely when life supporters, some of our closest family members, joined us. Brandon, and Megan, pregnant with their first child, came; Maggie, her husband, Mike, and their teenaged daughter, Kate, all came. Close friends, Bud and Cathy, visiting an elderly father in Florida, also joined us. In spite of the ongoing grief felt by everyone we drew close to each other, like campers around a fire. That was the best we could have done in December of 2002.

During our stay, I did have one encounter with Christmas. I passed a man walking down Duvall Street, the main street in the historic part of town. He was wearing shorts and a bright tropical shirt. Upon closer scrutiny I noticed that rather than parrots, the shirt had red Santa Clauses all over it. In fact he looked a little like Santa. After he passed me, I turned and photographed him. I guess that bright shirt brought out a bit of the elf in me despite my grief.

As I reflect back on our flight to Key West, my thoughts turn to Melissa and her love of the sun. Along the water front at the end of Duvall Street, there is an area with a long and colorful history called Mallory Square. That is a place that has always been known for its beautiful sunsets. However, in the 1800s it was also known for much pirate activity because this was where pirates anchored their ships. Much later, in the 1960s it was a place for LSD users to gather regularly to "watch Atlantis arising mythically out of the cloud formations at sunset" (Cultural Preservation Society, Key West, FL). About three decades ago, and up to the present, the "Sunset Celebration" in Mallory Square evolved into a dynamic gathering of artists of all kinds selling their work, along with those who wished to delight in the unsurpassed beauty of another sunset in paradise. I think Melissa would have loved that we spent our first Christmas without her in a place where it was warm and sunny during the daytime; and where we gathered with many others at the end of the day to feel a sense of wonder as our favorite star bid us good-night.

The powerful desire that John and I had initially felt, to disappear during the holidays, gradually began to diminish over the years. Emotionally, this was a much-needed relief. However, during this phase, the primary satisfaction was to be with our families and to accept quiet invitations from friends. It was a few more years before we rallied motivation to reciprocate and to resurrect our traditions.

Four years after Melissa died I made my first weak attempt to have a Christmas tree. I confiscated a small, artificial, pre-decorated tree that my mother had thrown out. I'm not even sure why I had salvaged it. After removing it from a plastic bag, I straightened out its tiny wire branches and planted it on a serving cart in the dining room. The thing stood about twenty-four inches high. It was hardly the freshly cut, full-sized tree that I usually set up in the most visible corner of the living room. But the effort was more than I had managed the year before. At the time I thought that I was doing pretty well by acknowledging the holidays at all.

One evening Brandon and his family came over for dinner. As we finished our meal, he looked at the tree and then at me and smiled. My interpretation—nothing was said—was that he found the tree to be a bit humorous, verging on pathetic. I felt a little sheepish, but had no intention of removing it.

The next year Brandon asked me, "Are you going to put up a tree this year?" Obviously last year's attempt hadn't counted. Immediately I thought, *Why bother?!* Then I felt his question as a gentle nudge. I began to think, *Why not?* It wasn't long before John and I went out, bought a full-sized tree and put it up in the living room. The tree was far from perfect. It was a little short and had two main branches at the top creating a fork. I camouflaged its flaw as best as I could with ribbon and the glittery star that Brandon had made in preschool.

By December of the sixth year I didn't wait for any prompting. We went out to the Christmas tree lot, bought a tree with a straighter shape and together we set it up. I took more pride in this one. After winding the tiny colored lights around and around—not my favorite decorating task—and, silently cursing the ones that remained dark, I began to feel more creative. I started having fun as I hung ornaments and draped wide strips of gold ribbon that glittered in the lights. I took my time. I breathed in the aroma of pine sap. Soon the tree glowed in a variety of colors and reflected light. As my vision bounced from one glistening ornament to another, some purple, aqua, and even lime green, I felt pleasure. My tree's look was not perfectly designed or expensively decorated. It certainly didn't look like something from a page in *Martha Stewart Living* magazine. What mattered was that I had enjoyed myself, using whatever creativity my limited talents allowed. That was my reward.

I have learned that grief is soothed by doing simple, engaging things. The mind calms itself and focuses. The heart beats at a nice regular rhythm. The body moves comfortably as a whole. Trimming my tree brought temporary peace to my spirit. It also helped stir pleasure into the month when I was more vulnerable to my grief; like adding cream and sugar to a bitter cup of coffee.

After ten years, I can say I am glad that John and I didn't succumb to our urge to leave town each December. We have remained every Christmas after the first one. This was because we had our son, his family, and other loving people for whom to stay home. It has meant that we needed to face, rather than avoid, the most savage dates of the year, that we have had to tolerate being targets of our own miserable memories, and that we needed to accept ourselves smiling and laughing when it seemed as though we shouldn't be. I learned that on some days I would still feel frozen inside as though an icy finger were pointing at me. At those times I believed that I would never thaw. Another day, the sun would appear, creating a dynamic flow to my life again, reminding me that everything changes.

35

Clumsy Encounter

In March of 2009, we spent spring break on an island in the Caribbean. Although I had been on the island a few years before, I had forgotten that winds can tear through this paradise, just like any other place, stirring up a lot of trouble for those living and vacationing there. Swells on the open water reached for the sky, playing no favorites with those in their paths. Waves crushed and pulverized the white coral beaches, rendering them cloudy and dangerous. That was the time riptides slithered into the shallows, luring an unknowing or unwise swimmer into terrifyingly deep water. Aquamarine colors of a sea in paradise could easily become those of a burial shroud.

One evening we decided to go on a sunset sail and had been instructed to wait for the captain in a little park across from the marina where his sailboat was moored. We wondered if he would cancel the "sunset and champagne sail" because of the rolling seas. Given the height of the waves, John and I had privately told each other that we wouldn't mind if the trip was cancelled. As we waited, we met the four other passengers. One of the women and her husband had previously sailed with the captain. The woman seemed especially friendly and extroverted, asking questions of everyone, soaking up information like a super-absorbent paper towel. She was short, a little stocky, with curly hair springing loosely around her smiling, inquisitive face. Her mascara had strayed from the intended fringe of her eyelashes. It was impossible to control makeup in warm, humid climates such as this, though she had obviously tried.

As soon as the captain appeared he assured us that the trip was a go and that we would be leaving shortly. We started to feel more comfortable and decided to view this as an adventure. Little did I know that before becoming tossed about by ocean waves, I would become emotionally unmoored by unexpected intrusions into my grief.

After introductions, we chatted for a few minutes with the captain. He told us that during the last year he had developed cancer in one of his eyes and his eye had been removed. I heard myself softly groan and noticed the sympathetic grimace on John's face. The woman listened and then offered a positive spin to the event with almost appropriate timing. She then briefly told of her own life-threatening story of the past few months. Hers had come to a miraculous resolution. So she, too, had suffered. I saw none of the pain behind her buttery smile. I felt judgmental and annoyed. I wanted to say, "Don't do that to me. Don't divert my attention away from the captain's pain before I'm ready. Don't tell me about your suffering and then quickly switch it off so there is no time for my feelings." From where I was standing, this wasn't a one-way street. In my case, after nine years of missing Melissa, I had much to talk about. But I was very selective as to whom, where, what, and when I did so. Listening to the captain and the woman made me uncomfortable. In one way I envied the apparent ease with which they openly talked about their serious health problems.

The sunny, inquisitive woman and I walked to the skiff together. She had mentioned earlier that she had an adult son who had not been able to join her and her husband this year on the island holiday. She asked me, "Do you have any children, or have you chosen not to?" Inside myself I paused, distracted by this oddly phrased question. She seemed to be trying hard to sound politically correct. I thought, maybe her extroversion wiggles its way into so many lives that she has learned to be careful how she speaks. I said, "Yes, I have" . . . now my heart beat a little faster.

I anticipated her next question and began to consider my response. I could feel her bobbing in closer to my most personal wound. I felt defiant. I refused to let her hook me, although I was unsure about how much information I wanted to give in this setting, with her and at this time. This little woman, over whom I loomed by at least six inches, posed a threat by her everyday inquiries. Even though I wanted the caring and support of others, I had to quickly assess what and how much I wanted this stranger to know. I owed her nothing. I could even make something up. I could say I was barren, which would fit neither of the categories she presented. Yes, my hackles stood up like a hostile hound dog's. I told her, "I have a son" and elaborated a bit about his family. I could have stopped there, but I continued, "And, a daughter who is deceased." I thought, "I will not save you from the pain of my life."

She remained undaunted. I should have guessed. She asked, "Was she young . . . ?"

I answered, "She was twenty-five."

"How did she die?"

I assessed my vulnerability and I knew exactly how much information I would give. She was on my leash now. I told her, "She had a cardiac arrest." This yellow t-shirted woman in khaki shorts with long pearly pink nails, who had known terror herself, even though I couldn't detect it, empathically acknowledged that this must have been hard. I said, "It was incredibly bad." I didn't elaborate. There would be no more talk of this. As we left the pain behind, we moved into the safe topic of grandchildren. It felt like a fountain spraying me with cool, pure water.

Our attention turned to the captain as we boarded his sailing vessel. After a few instructions, he took us out to sea. We kept our eyes on the wind-driven waves. We sipped champagne, nibbled at cheese and swallowed the cool juice of grapes as we plucked them from their stems. We frequently checked the progress of the sun as it dropped closer and closer towards the darkening waves. In the end, clouds in the west disappointed our hoped-for sunset. Yet, when I turned to look toward the harbor, I discovered a white marble moon in an inky night sky.

Looking back on my strong reaction and internal confusion triggered by the woman in yellow, I can see that I need to challenge myself to talk more frequently with others who cared about Melissa. I need to ask them to tell me stories and memories they have about her. Telling myself to take these risks sounds so reasonable, and yet, when I'm in an actual social situation it feels like an iron door slams shut in my chest making it impossible to speak. Obviously, I have more grief work to do.

36

Family Changes

In the spring of 1995 Brandon and his fiancée Megan graduated from college and were married one week later. Since Melissa attended the same college, she often hung out with them during her freshman year, the one year their attendance overlapped. As a result, she and Megan got to know each other well. Even though Brandon and Megan moved out of Minnesota twice during the next several years to work and attend school, Melissa visited them and maintained her relationship with them. Once they returned to the Twin Cities to live, family events and shared experiences grew into an even deeper common history. On the morning Melissa died, Megan, Brandon, John, and I stood together around her bed.

Although Brandon and Megan's marriage ended several years after Melissa's death, they had presented us with our first grandchildren and continued to have a shared parental relationship. Two years later Brandon married Ashley. Melissa and Ashley had never known each other and because she was new to our family there was no common history. Anything that Ashley knew about Melissa was secondhand. They hadn't hung out at college together or shared funny stories at family gatherings. They had never gone shopping or discussed things they were passionate about. The days of crisis and raw grief were over by the time Brandon and Ashley met. There was just white space where experience with Melissa was concerned.

I found myself wanting to fill some of that space by talking about Melissa with Ashley. I wanted to do this in a way that would feel as natural and comfortable as possible. I decided to try to build a bridge that all of us could use within the family whenever we needed to. Although Ashley was already an important part of our lives, it felt as though we would be folding her more completely into our family if we included Melissa.

John and I made use of grief therapy as we worked on this. It wasn't because this was something severely painful for us but more because we felt unsettled by it. Whenever our family structure changed in some way it created new challenges in how to deal with grief. More specifically, Melissa's death, directly or indirectly, had an impact on everyone in the family. For example, when an important anniversary date arrived, such as her death date or birthday, feelings rippled throughout the family. Together, John and I decided that, with Brandon and Ashley, we would conduct a simple ritual to introduce our new daughter-in-law to our daughter.

On a November Sunday morning Brandon and Ashley rang the doorbell. Ashley held a bouquet of mums in my favorite color, burnt red. Bringing flowers was the perfect touch. They smiled. We smiled. First, we caught up on their daily life, which John and I always found interesting. I took extra time arranging the mums in a large glass vase, placing the larger mums behind the smaller ones. I fussed with it a bit, trying to cut the stems just the right length. The arrangement was important because it was for Melissa. I placed the flowers on the table. They would adorn the simple ritual we had planned. We would place a small amount of Melissa's ashes into the bottom of a wooden sculpture that we had commissioned an artist to design just for this purpose.

We began informally by sharing several sets of photographs that we had set up in another part of the room. We knew that Ashley had never seen the beautiful enlarged photographs that Melissa's friends had put together for her memorial service. Each foam board also held a quote from someone Melissa admired. Taking our time we looked at each one. There was a large black-and-white one taken by Brandon for a high school photography class. In it Melissa appeared uncharacteristically serious, yet she looked into the lens with clarity and directness. It had always made her seem so alive to me and was especially meaningful because Brandon took it. She was about thirteen-years-old at the time. As we moved from one set to another, different realms of Melissa's life were depicted. One set included childhood scenes. Her friends had selected a quote from Ani DiFranco.

As we continued looking at more photographs of friends, travels, and family, we would pause at times to ask, "Where exactly was that one taken?" As we peered at one series of photos of Melissa as a young adult, Brandon briefly tattled on her, informing us that she smoked cigarettes more than we knew. Another story had to do with a party Melissa was planning to attend. Supposedly, illegal substances were going to be used. She, of course, was not even close to twenty-one. It was to be a high school end-of-senior-year celebration. When Brandon told us about this at the time, I informed her she couldn't attend. For months after that, Melissa was mad at Brandon for tattling on her. I have no idea what went on at that party—or even if it happened—however, it was an example of the kind of story I expected to hear years later from both of my kids as they got older.

I loved tales like these that parents only hear after the fact, after all potential danger was avoided. In this case it was rather unfair because Melissa did not have a chance to defend herself or retaliate. Talking as we were, I was reminded of the lively dynamic between our children. It was also a powerful reminder of how, for twenty-five years, Brandon had a younger sister whose life wove in and out of his own, how she had made many of her life choices because he, her big brother, had already scouted out the path making it more familiar and less daunting, and how they had understood and admired each other so very much.

We told a few more family stories as we continued through the brief photo history. As Ashley listened attentively, I felt more and more comfortable. Emotionally, she seemed to be up to the task, standing beside us, graciously allowing us to bring her closer to Melissa, our daughter, Brandon's sister, her deceased sister-in-law, whom she could never meet directly yet who continued to have a presence in our family.

The foam boards with rectangular cutouts framing the photographs seemed like miniature doors that opened up another room of our lost Melissa's life. Each one we entered allowed us, in the present, to meet her again in the past. Even though it was impossible for Ashley to have any living experiences with Melissa, perhaps a relationship could grow through greater ease in talking about her, and having a stronger base of memories and stories.

We left the photographs and turned our attention to the wooden sculpture standing erect on the table. It had been carved out of padouk, a tree native to central and tropical Africa. Smooth to the touch, the dark wooden shape extended upwards like a female form turning and stretching unafraid. Eighteen inches tall, it also communicated balance, youth, and openness with abstract, arced wings ready for flight. Patterns in the dark grain moved in circles and waves throughout the sculpture so that one's eyes were kept in motion. Yet the simplicity of its shape and a warm light reflected by its luster soothed the spirit. Beneath the wood was an ivory marble base that sat atop a wooden base. It is here that a hollow space was carved to house a small portion of Melissa's ashes.

I laid a new white linen towel under the sculpture. It seemed imperative that we not spill any ash or, if we did, we must deal with it in a respectful way. Since we didn't have any prescribed ritual for dealing with a mishap, we found ourselves being very careful.

I slipped the small cardboard box out of the plain white paper bag with small handles. I opened it from the end that was labeled, "The Cremated Remains of Melissa Maureen Sullivan." Since I had seen Melissa's ashes one other time when we scattered some of them high above the North Shore of Lake Superior, I felt slightly more prepared. John had a spoon ready with which to scoop small amounts of ash. Holding the sculpture upside down we took turns. As I filled my spoonful, I noticed the variation in color and texture of the ash. I was prepared this time for the small, white shards of bone. Only briefly did I pause, allowing the truth that these were the remains, the bones of my daughter.

Days before I had wondered if this intimate ritual would bring me to my knees in tears. Did I feel sorrow, heavily suspended deep within me? Absolutely. After several years did I cry? Not often visibly but frequently on the inside. What I have found is that often when my tears come they are triggered by the unexpected. A couple of days before, while shopping, I had seen a mother and a little daughter whose blond hair was cut in a pixie style popular in the late 70s. There I stood in the brightly lit store, the rims of my eyes starting to burn. The tears of yearning felt like acid.

We tightly screwed the bottom onto the sculpture. Then we set the lovely form upright. The ashes were held securely. Sometime in the future we will give the sculpture to Brandon and his family. Finally, I allowed myself to openly invite Ashley and Brandon to talk with John and me about Melissa then and in the future. I felt as though a bridge to Melissa had been constructed, one that could be crossed by any one of us anytime we needed to. With a sense of fullness, the ritual seemed complete.

Now it was time for breakfast. Ashley and Brandon did the cooking. I let them, feeling a little tired, finding that it felt very good to have them take care of me in that way.

37

Say Her Name

As December 2010 approached, I still felt as though time was bullying me, forcing me to rip November from the calendar before I was ready. Why should I want to move into the month in which I spent the worst twelve days of my life? Why should I want to see those vivid images that threatened the calm, which, at least externally, I maintained much of the time; and which sliced into me like sharp knives. Soon I would start digging in my heels in my usual desperate, yet futile attempt to slow down time. Once December started and I surrendered to the fact that I couldn't stop the days from passing, I would be able to think of the first thirteen days as normal. But all the days that followed I would designate as ones in which I felt vulnerable, ones through which I had to walk softly. I had been through this routine nine times and was pretty sure that this was how it would go, and that I might even have some nice times scattered throughout the second half of the month.

One more specific fear began to nag at me that year. I was afraid that no one, or very few, would mention Melissa's name, recount a past memory, or refer to her in any way. For some reason, my desire to talk about her with others had intensified this year. I began to feel desperate. I predicted that the light that once radiated brightly from Melissa's personality and very active life would slant and cool like a winter's sun, that her full twenty-five years would be reduced to a string of twelve tragic days in December. I knew our supporters still cared. I reminded myself that almost a decade had passed since her death. Our tragedy was not, nor should it be, the focal point of others' lives. Eventually, I came to the realization that I should not expect others to anticipate what my needs were, unless I let them know. My unease continued, however.

I had really gotten ahead of myself as I worried about a December yet to come. It was still November, the day after Thanksgiving, the morning of the annual "Decorate the Christmas Tree Party" at Brandon and Ashley's house. They began this warm tradition at the same time they were blending their families. Since each brought two children from their previous relationships, there would be a total of four and an equal number of grandparents joining Brandon and Ashley for this seasonal family ritual. It would be a lively time, as the children, seven-years-old and younger, unleashed their excitement and creativity on the Christmas tree.

John and I loved this party because it was a day we could count on to keep us close to others as we came closer to our worst time of the year. John would also think of Melissa and feel sad that she was missing out in so many ways, especially by not having met her nieces and nephews.

Two bins loaded with ornaments were brought up from the basement. The tree with pre-strung white lights stood very importantly in a prime corner as if waiting to be dressed for the party. Brandon and Ashley carefully opened the red bins with green covers. Nevertheless, as soon as the children spotted the contents, ornaments began tumbling out, with some landing on the floor, but none breaking. Each child became totally engrossed with the ornament they held and hung. Sometimes one of us would tell a little story about a specific ornament or ask a question about its origins. "Do you remember when your grandmother made that one for you?" "This was your first ornament." The children, completely unaware, continued to create new memories with each additional ornament they hung on the tree.

For several years when Brandon and Melissa were young, I gave each of them a new ornament that I expected they would take with them when they became adults. After Melissa died I gave most of hers to Brandon. I watched as my four-year-old granddaughter selected two of them. They were white plastic discs. One was a boy and a dog and the other was a girl and a cat. Smiling, she announced, "These are Daddy's and Missy's." I hesitated, noticing a familiar thump in my chest. *Let's move on*, I thought to myself. A few minutes later she picked up another ornament stating, "This one is Missy's. It's a green flamingo." In her clear four-year-old voice she communicated that this one was special, and she was happy that she got to hang it. It took me by surprise because I had forgotten about that ornament. It was indeed a three-inch-long, rather funky-looking bright-green wooden flamingo. I remembered it always made me smile and think about how funny Melissa could be.

Once the tree was completely "decked out" and the bins returned to the basement, the grandmothers gave a new ornament to each child, marking this year. The grandfathers wondered out loud where eight more could possibly go on the tree. The grandmothers ignored them and continued smiling at their grandchildren. All of the adults noticed how many more ornaments were found higher up this year because the kids had grown much taller. As I looked at the tree I realized how much family love and meaning were hanging from its branches, some of it past and some of it present. I also realized that each of these four children would have a fine collection of decorations to take with them when they were adults and had trees of their own and could tell their own stories.

Later that night, I kept hearing my granddaughter's voice saying, "This one is Missy's. It's a green flamingo." Why were those words echoing in my head? As I allowed the words to sink deeper I noticed how they touched a vulnerable spot, that familiar ache. When my granddaughter spoke "Missy's" name out loud, she let it be known that, even though Melissa was gone, and even though she had never met her aunt, she could bring her presence to life by imagining her and speaking her name. My four-year-old granddaughter had broken through my icy defenses, allowing me to feel my sadness and to breathe more easily. She had given me a priceless gift to take with me into December, the hardest month of the year.

38

Channeling Melissa

Four days before Christmas 2010, John's sister Maggie called. "John, I have something to tell you," she said gravely. He immediately leaped to all sorts of terrifying scenarios. Maggie had his full attention as he waited for her to go on. What she said next was, "Your niece is about to become your nephew." After that he primarily listened, trying to digest the information he was hearing. Once his sister had finished and had hung up the phone, John filled me in about the news. Only then did we let our reactions loose. Our feelings flew around the room like cornered bats. Questions piled on top of one another, some rational, some based on ignorance, while others were expressions of sheer emotion.

After we had had more time to absorb the stunning news we began to feel very protective towards our niece who was in transition to become our nephew. Even though she was in her middle twenties, at our age, she seemed very young and we wondered whether she was equipped to make such an enormous decision and to experience such a profound metamorphosis. There was never any doubt that John and I would accept and support her. But we lacked experience with this kind of transition. We worried about many aspects of it, including the impact it would have on her partner, Meghan, of whom we had become very fond.

Two days after the phone call, John and I, his sister, our niece-in-transition and Meghan, and Brandon and Ashley had dinner prior to attending a dance performance. During our time together our niece spoke quite openly about the decisions she was beginning to make, answering as many of our questions as she could at the time. Everyone listened supportively.

The following day Brandon and Ashley came over to our house to do some final holiday bread baking for Christmas Eve. While the four of us were gathered in the kitchen, I asked Brandon and Ashley what they thought of the news from the previous evening. Neither showed a strong reaction and took the news calmly in stride. They were accepting and supportive. Their mild, brief responses surprised me, and kind of shut me up.

Then Brandon looked at me with a wry smile on his face and said, "You should channel Missy." I loved to hear this for two reasons. One was that he had brought up his sister's name. He didn't do this often. The second reason I loved this was that he remembered and reminded me how open Melissa was about social norms and how she had introduced us many times to worlds beyond the rather limiting one in which we lived most of the time.

Immediately after graduating from college, Melissa and one of her roommates who happened to be gay decided to get jobs in Minneapolis and share an apartment. Her roommate had not "come out" to many others or to his family. During that year they often got together with other friends, straight and gay, and as a group started frequenting the Gay 90's, a "gay" bar. I'm sure Melissa enjoyed watching my eyes get wider and wider, as she told me that they had made friends with the Drag Queen and how nice "she" was. Although I never felt that I fully understood this, she and her friends, straight and gay, clearly felt comfortable in this community. I believe that one of the initial motivations for going to that particular bar was trying to help her friend feel more comfortable as a gay young man.

When Brandon suggested that I "channel Missy" it actually allowed me to do so. As I reached back in time I could appreciate qualities that I loved about her. She was playful and helpful, thoughtful, loyal, and open-minded. When it came to her parents, she liked to push the envelope, nudging us to examine what we thought were already open and liberal beliefs. So even though she wasn't standing in front of us with a big smile on her face and an arm draped around her brother, I had the strong sense that together they were challenging us to open our eyes and lighten up!

39

Return of Joy

I always knew that I would love to be a grandmother. However, I never expected that it would be magical. The magic turned out to be the return of moments of joy! This was an emotion that I thought I had lost forever. The ability to feel pleasure and satisfaction at times had gradually returned, but it seemed unrealistic to expect to feel the ultimate emotional high of joy.

My first grandchild was born in 2003. Looking down at my grandson's tiny round baby face as I laid him on my lap—barely touching the silky hair on the top of his head, making his eyes flutter with sleepiness—was magical. The joy I felt continued to grow along with him and multiplied three years later when my granddaughter was born.

After Brandon remarried, I became a step-grandmother for a step-granddaughter and a step-grandson. It was as if Flora, Fauna, and Merryweather, the good fairies from "Sleeping Beauty," had waved their wands at me. My relationship with these four children seemed to hold special power, fortifying me against the hopelessness of loss.

It should not be surprising that perched at the top of my list of greatest pleasures are my four grandchildren: Ailish, Wynn, Ian, and Kieran, from youngest to oldest. Like tiny stealth fliers, they easily pass through my defenses. Encircling my heart, they come in close and land. Facing them I grin. Then we all throw our arms around each other. Each time we meet, I feel more confident as I move into my future. The hugs, the kisses, the love, are exchanged with complete abandon. They give me so much. I hope their lives are enriched by having me in theirs as well. As I look at their sweet beauty, I try not to think about how love makes us hopelessly vulnerable to loss.

When one's child dies the loss shatters like flying shrapnel, throughout every season, every holiday, every event, and relationship— it becomes part of who you are. It settles in your bones. The experience kills a part of you.

Nevertheless, I have one last thought to share. After a time, when survival seems possible, if you feel like plugging your nose and jumping into life like a kid into a swimming hole, then swing out far and jump in with gusto. If you feel like wearing a black cloak all day and speaking to no one, do it. The choice to act in accordance with how you feel is one way to honor your grief and loss. Each of us, against our will, has become part of a tight group, invisibly bonded, because of this loss. Privately, we know we'd ditch this crowd in a heartbeat if we could have our loved one back. But we know that's not going to happen.

Human beings suffer in more ways than any one of us can imagine. And it is impossible to live on this planet very long without partaking in some form of sorrow. Each story of loss is unique and each person is invaluable. Those of us who have lost a child know that each day we live is another day we have earned our stripes by staring down tragedy. We also know that doesn't make us heroes. It is each and every life supporter, who chose to come close to us in our misery, that I call courageous and for whom I hold enormous gratitude.

Grief Tale: Two

The woman in the forest who had lost her daughter lived so long it seemed to her as though several lifetimes had passed. She still had her comfortable little house in a clearing in the woods. The river still emptied into the small lake surrounded by berry bushes. Her husband still had a twinkle in his eye when he kissed her cheek. Friends of many years, though fewer of them now, lived nearby. Her hip hurt and her eyesight depended on specially made thick glasses. Yet, most of the time life was pleasant even though she and her companions hobbled a bit. The woman appreciated simple things like the sun, which allowed pink petunias and lacy white alyssum to grow in flowerboxes in front of her house. She also felt pleasure observing the birds and animals that happened to wander through her clearing in the woods.

Never a day went by that she did not miss her daughter. On the mantelpiece atop the stone fireplace were framed photographs of her at different ages. The woman thought they were beautiful, and yet, she limited the length of time she gazed at any one of them. Sometimes, when no one else was around, she took off her specially made thick glasses to make her vision blurry as she looked at the pictures. This way she kept her daughter at a distance and pretended the worst had not happened.

She felt sad, reminding herself that this was how it would be for the rest of her life. She worried that the dark thoughts might once again worm their way into her mind: thoughts of death and how it would bring an end to the ache she had felt so long. "If only something could magically bring me relief," she thought. She remembered all the fairy tales she had read to her grandchildren when they were little, and how the good fairies with their wands could fix almost anything. But she knew better.

One day when the woman was feeling sad, she decided to try to cheer herself up with a cup of tea. She put on the kettle and sat down in her rocking chair to wait. Removing her glasses, she placed them in her lap while she rested her eyes. Quickly she fell asleep and slipped into a dream. The first thing she saw was a beautiful hand-carved clock on the mantel. Her husband had given it to her for her last birthday. It was a special clock: instead of minute and hour hands, it had one large hand that marked the passage of a year. Her husband said that if she turned the hand counterclockwise she could travel back in time. That had made her so happy. "Now I can visit my daughter!" she thought. It seemed odd that she had never used the clock before now.

The woman walked to the mantel. She took hold of the large hand and turned it back one year for every year her daughter had been gone. Then she stopped and waited for her daughter to appear. Suddenly her husband walked in and immediately realized what she had done. He fell to his knees with an expression of agony on his face. "Do you realize that whatever year you have turned the hand to, that will be the one in which you will live forever? Anything that has happened since, or would have happened in the future, will be lost to you." The woman did not know what to do. She knew what this meant. She felt a deep pain in her heart. She became so filled with fear and sorrow and anger that she let out a piercing scream.

She awoke with her arms flailing and the tea kettle whistling. Her specially made thick glasses flew onto the stone hearth shattering into many pieces. "My glasses!" she moaned, "My eyes!" Because she lived so far from the nearest village she knew that it might be weeks before she got a new pair. The woman got down on her knees and collected as much of the glass as she could feel with her hands. When she stood up, she was in front of her favorite picture of her daughter. As hard as she tried to see it, all she saw was a blurry image. The woman felt quite depressed. Her specially made thick glasses had allowed her to see her daughter's face clearly and to feel her alive again. The woman wondered how she could have forgotten—or tried to forget—the importance of staying close to her child even though she couldn't be with her.

In all the upheaval, the woman had forgotten that it was Sunday afternoon, the time of the week when her son, his wife, and their four children came to visit.

The children were big now. All of them were taller than her and her husband. As soon as they arrived and walked into the living room, her oldest grandson said, "Grandma, you look sad." The woman told everyone what had happened. "Well," he said, "we're here now!" Given that he was the oldest grandchild, he announced, "Let's each do something to make Grandma and Grandpa happy." Together the granddaughters danced, arms interlaced, as they sang their favorite songs. Next, the younger grandson made them laugh out loud when he dropped tiny toads from the forest into their laps; and, finally the oldest grandson took them on a boat ride across the lake and back so they could feel the gentle breeze and feel the warm sun all around them.

When they got back to the house, her husband made tea and served everyone bowls of freshly picked berries with thick cool cream. As they sat enjoying the late summer treats, the woman was able to catch up on news from her son and daughter-in-law's lives. She was so proud of both of them and loved hearing details about their family and work activities and plans. For a while, as her son was talking in his steady voice interspersed with a wry sense of humor, she stopped listening and just gazed at him. "My son," she thought, "I am so lucky!"

As her son, her daughter-in-law, and their four children were hugging their "good-byes," the woman looked at each one of them and said, "You have made this a wonderful day." The oldest said, "Remember, we'll be back next Sunday afternoon." As the woman shut the door her heart felt as full as it could get.

"Tomorrow I shall order a new pair of glasses," she said to her husband. As he got ready to sit down in his own rocking chair, she added, "I'd love to have a fire tonight, and perhaps, you would read to me for a little while from my book?"

He looked at her and said, "It would be my pleasure." Then he kissed her on the cheek, his eye twinkled and he went to get the firewood.

The End

This book has come to an end.
The story has not.

Appendix

Dos and Don'ts for Life Supporters

The following is a brief guide of "dos and don'ts" for those who want to be more effective supporters of bereaved parents. The list is not comprehensive nor is it intended to fit every grieving parent. Keep in mind the following:

1. Grief's intensity evolves very slowly.
2. Expectations and support must adapt accordingly.
3. Bereaved parents react in typical as well as unique ways to their loss.
4. Consider any circumstance regarding the child's death that might complicate it and thus compromise the parents' abilities to cope.
5. As a caring person, you will want to eliminate the parents' pain—remember that it is impossible to do so and that any such attempts may paradoxically interfere with their grieving.

DO anticipate the most important things a griever might need.

DON'T take action without briefly checking with them first.

DO ask, suggest, or offer.

DON'T tell or take over.

DO remember (especially early on) that the bereaved are vulnerable and emotionally overloaded.

DON'T patronize them.

DO understand that not only do the circumstances surrounding a child's death create extraordinary pain, but there may be other factors that complicate it. (Parents, for example, often blame themselves for not having protected their child.)

DON'T ask a lot of questions regarding the circumstances surrounding the death. Over time you will be told as much as the parents are ready to tell.

DO allow the parents to express their feelings and have their tears. It is helpful to them when someone listens in a caring way.

DON'T expect that you should have profound words of comfort.

DO give them plenty of time to talk. This is unlike any other conversation.

DON'T be critical of yourself if you feel uncomfortable with their grief. Just listen and/or do what you can, when you can. Being "up close and personal" is not for everyone.

DO understand that the intolerable pain following the death of a child lasts a long time. Even after it decreases and is tolerated, the pain will continue for the rest of the parents' life. It is never too late to show your support.

DON'T expect that even your best efforts to be supportive will bring a quick or noticeable change in their emotions.

DO recognize that the bereaved are the experts of their own grief. They are having an experience only shared by other bereft parents.

DON'T offer advice, platitudes, or say things such as, "You can't run away from it"; "Just don't think about it"; "It will take time." In addition, be cautious with the words "healing" and "recovery."

DO respect the fact that parents have different beliefs as to what happened to their child following their death.

DON'T assume or indicate that everyone believes, or should believe what you do.

DO suggest professional help if you have valid concerns that the parent has become destructive to themselves or someone else. Also, assist them in any way you can to set up the contact.

DON'T try to do grief counseling.

DO invite a parent out for a low-stress activity or offer to visit them in their home shortly after their child's loss. They will tell you if they are not ready. Avoid feeling offended. It was right to ask. Try again later.

DON'T discourage yourself by thinking that simple visits or caring gestures are not important. They are all valuable because you are helping them construct a new future through a normal daily interaction and possibly interrupting their pain for a short time.

DO remain constant in the parent's life, whether through spontaneous or regular contact. Also, remember that anniversary days, such as the child's birthday or day of their death are extremely poignant and can be a good time to show a gesture of support.

DON'T stop having contact with the parent after the first few weeks or even months. Visits and contact initiated by others often taper off too soon and can feel like another loss to the griever.

DO know that if you have had a relationship with the deceased child, you affirm and honor them when you have contact with their parents. Also, you may discover that it helps you to see and talk with them.

DON'T stay away because you are afraid of their sadness or yours. They are supposed to feel sadness as well as many other feelings, and so are you.

Prior to applying any of these "Dos and Don'ts" it is important to consider how far along in the grief process the parents are, how close your relationship to them is, and how open to others they seem to be. If you aren't clear about any of these, proceed cautiously, but DO proceed.

Bibliography

American Psychiatric Association. 1994. *Desk Reference to the Diagnostic and Statistical Manual of Mental Disorders from the DSM-IV-TR.* Washington, DC: American Psychiatric Association.

Carroll, Lewis. *Alice's Adventures in Wonderland and Through the Looking-Glass.* New York: Barnes & Noble Books, 2004.

Cather, Willa. *My Antonia.* New York: Penguin Putnam, Inc. 1994.

Cranford, Ronald E. and Raymond Gensinger. "Hospital Policy on Terminal Sedation and Euthanasia," *HEC Forum* 14(3), (2002) 259-264.

Croll, Jillian, Dianne Neumark-Sztainer, Mary Story, and Marjorie Ireland, "Prevalence and risk and protective factors related to disordered eating behaviors among adolescents: relationship to gender and ethnicity." *Journal of Adolescent Health* 31 (2002): 166-175.

Didion, Joan. *The Year of Magical Thinking.* New York: Alfred A. Knopf, 2005.

Fossum, Karin. *Black Seconds.* New York: Houghton Mifflin Harcourt, 2009.

Klass, Dennis, "The Deceased Child in the Psychic and Social Worlds of Bereaved Parents During the Resolution of Grief." *Continuing Bonds: New Understandings of Grief,* edited by Dennis Klass, Phyllis R. Silverman, and Steven L. Nickman, 199-215. Philadelphia: Taylor & Francis, 1996.

Krieger, Derk W. "Evoked Potentials Not Just to Confirm Hopelessness in Anoxic Brain Injury," *The Lancet* 352(9143), (1998) 1796-1797.

Lynch, Thomas. *The Undertaking: Life Studies from the Dismal Trade.* New York: Penguin Group, 1998.

McCauley, Barbara. *Small Mercies.* Santa Fe, NM: Sherman Asher Publishing, 1998.

McGovern, George. Terry. *My Daughter's Life-and-Death Struggle with Alcoholism.* New York: Plume, published by Penguin Group, 1997.

The Multi-Society Task Force on PVS. "Medical Aspects of the Persistent Vegetative State," *N Engl J Med* 330 (1994): 1499-1508.

Novotney, Amy, "New Solutions," *Monitor on Psychology* 40 (2009): 47-51.

Rando, Therese A., Ph.D. *How To Go On Living When Someone You Love Dies.* New York: Bantam edition, 1991.

Simmons, Philip. *Learning To Fall: The Blessings of an Imperfect Life.* New York: Bantam Books, 2002.

Acknowledgments

I want to thank Patricia Francisco for her sensitive, patient and sustained encouragement without which this book would not have come to fruition. She challenged my writing and provided invaluable feedback over the course of several years. A professor and published author of several books, Patricia Francisco served as my coach and was a constant inspiration.

I also want to thank my husband, John, who in 2002 shared my intense desire to write a book that we hoped would be helpful to others. During the first year this was a joint writing endeavor, however, after John needed to turn his attention to his professional life, I continued on my own. John remained a constant support from the sidelines and encouraged me in every way.

Patti Frazee, project manager for the book, deserves full credit for having prepared this book for self-publishing in print and for e-publishing. Her effectiveness, efficiency and excellent follow-through have been greatly appreciated.

Enormous thanks go to several people who took the time to critically read the book and give me honest input. Their fresh perspectives and ideas led to important improvements. They are: Lee Bradford, Nancy Foster, Joel Hetler, Ashley Mercer, Ellen Sampson, Martin Sampson, Julie Schumacher, Tom Skovholt, Brandon Sullivan, and Patricia West.

In addition, I want to specifically thank Gene Borgida for generously and personally introducing me to the world of agents and publishing.

I must reiterate the profound gratitude I have for all who became part of our community of supporters over a decade ago. The power of that support is what continuously fed my determination to finish the book.

Finally, in addition to John, without whom I fear I could not have endured the loss of Melissa, I have been sustained in my endeavor by the love and caring of family and friends. Our son and his wife, Brandon and Ashley, and their children, our grandchildren—Ailish, Wynn, Ian and Kieran—have made my life full, and I am thankful for them every day.

About the Author

Judith Sullivan grew up in southern Minnesota, received a B.A. degree from the University of Minnesota, a M.A. in Counseling Psychology from the University of St. Thomas and has worked at a major urban hospital in Minneapolis as a psychologist for many years. Since her daughter's death in 2001, she has written about her bereavement as it evolved over a decade. Profoundly affected by specific forms of support received throughout this experience, she was inspired to write this book and share these life-enhancing lessons with others.

CPSIA information can be obtained at www.ICGtesting.com
Printed in the USA
LVOW04s1654290115

424894LV00013B/553/P